DEDICATION

To Ian Love, without whom nobody would be reading this.

LIGHT-HEARTED SPEECHMAKING

by

Duncan Gillespie

The Amateur Winemaker,
South Street, Andover, Hants.

1st IMPRESSION 1972

ISBN 0 900841 27 3

Printed in Great Britain by:
The Standard Press (Andover) Ltd., South Street, Andover, Hants.
Telephone: 2413

Chapter Headings

". . face the folk out there in the Woodyard . . ."

Why Speak at All?

When this volume was in the making, a friend said to me, "Oh, you're writing a book about public speaking? I'm sure it will impress anyone who has not heard you make a speech!"

I suppose my feelings should have been hurt, but I saw what he meant. If your mental image of the ideal public speaker is the Golden-Tongue Orator who looks as if he had come straight out of a bandbox, who says nothing in a mid-Atlantic accent in beautifully rounded sentences, and who ends up finding fame and fortune by conning his boss into giving him his daughter's hand in marriage and a half-share in The Company . . . well, I'm not him.

If you would prefer to be the kind of speaker who can get up on a platform without stumbling with nervousness, can face the folk out there in the Woodyard and know that they are your friends, can earn the interest of the audience and gain a few laughs, and can come down afterwards to deserved applause then this book may be of some use to you.

You may even come to share my enjoyment of public speaking—an enjoyment that comes from the realisation that I am unique!

And so are you.

Whether you are an expert on treacle-mining in North Yorkshire (a subject which crops up from time to time in these pages) or are often called on to tell stories after dinner, this book is intended to help you to realise your own strong points, and to become a relaxed and easy speaker because you are not pretending to be someone else—not even the Golden-Tongued Orator.

If you are not already roped into speaking in public, now is the time to turn back. . . . There are plenty of reasons for not speaking in public. After all, if you avoid it you are less likely to come down with foot-in-mouth disease—a closed mouth gathers no feet.

If you do no public speaking, you have more time for other activities—unbroken evenings watching shadows speaking, instead of being out meeting real people.

And speaking is wearing. The stress of a ten-minute speech has been computed as equivalent to that of driving a racing car for five minutes.

Making any speech is like walking a tightrope—though generally a fairly broad tightrope. You must keep your balance between too formal and too informal a manner, between undue brevity and wearisome length, between broad accent and over-punctilious English, among the permissible shades of blue in jokes.

There is no reason, though, why you should not be eloquent in the best sense of the word—"True eloquence consists in saying all that is necessary, and nothing but what is necessary". If, like me, you have heard thousands of speeches, you can console yourself by thinking that while it is highly unlikely that you will make a speech to match the best you have ever heard, it is even more unlikely that you will make one to match the dull grey prosy speeches you have had to sit through.

And public speaking can have its rewards.

I think back to the afternoon I went to speak to a pensioners' organisation. My subject was none too serious, and I "hammed" the speech for all it was worth, and sat down soaked in sweat.

Someone sang "Love's Old Sweet Song", tea and biscuits were served, and then to my horror I heard the Chairman saying "We enjoyed the first half—we'll just have Mr. Gillespie back up on his feet for another half-hour."

I had to get up and, literally from cold, start afresh.

There was an old lady in the front row. Her face was drawn with long-familiar pain, and her leg was supported on front of her on a stool. Part of my reward was the knowledge that while I was up there hamming away she had forgotten all about her leg. Then I had to leave early. The Chairman called on a member to propose a vote of thanks—and while

I was outside and putting my coat on, they were still applauding. I was near to tears, knowing that those old people had done *me* a favour that afternoon.

It is a great feeling when your speech takes off like a surfboard and begins to move forward on a big sustaining wave of audience response; and it is intoxicating when you know that you have your audience in the hollow of your hand and that they are going to laugh when you want them to laugh, and dab their eyes when you want them to cry. It is a dangerous feeling too . . . perhaps it is just as well, before we all become demagogues, that it is tempered by the times when audiences laugh at exactly the wrong times, and yawn a little blatantly.

Sometimes, too, you are sure you have scored, then find that things were not quite as rosy as you thought.

I remember addressing an audience of teenagers on the

heroic example of the Polish nun who took the place of a young Jewess weeping in the queue for the gas-chambers in a concentration camp. Speaking with sincere admiration for this modern Christian martyr, I was happy to see on one young face in the audience an answering look of rapt attention.

Encouraged, I was fired to do better, only to find that when I stopped my address he still looked as attentive as ever. He was sitting with a small transistor radio plugged in to his left ear, and was listening to "Top of the Pops".

Some people are suspicious of eloquence, but the public speaker's ability is in itself neutral—it can be used to seduce or to strengthen, to heal or to hurt, to destroy or to amuse. And to convince, in a good or evil cause.

Back in 1622 Pope Gregory XV set up an organisation to spread the Faith throughout the world, and coined a word that has since acquired a very bad reputation. The organisation was the "Congregatio de propaganda fide"—and propaganda has come to mean the unscrupulous use of distorted facts to persuade people to do what you want them to do.

In the best use of the word, a well-made speech is in itself excellent propaganda, making your audience think well not only of you but of the organisation or cause you represent.

Do not be over-impressed by loud applause. Instead, after you have given a speech, take a few minutes to go over it in your head and think out what you did really well and what you did badly. Even if you do not note your conclusions down, or make any formal good resolutions, you will find that this afterthought helps you to avoid in future the mistakes you have spotted, and to remember to repeat the good points.

If you can listen to a good tape-recording of what you said you will find this a salutary help.

If you are acquainted with a reporter who has been covering the function, you ask him for his honest opinion. He has to listen professionally to hundreds of speeches a year, and if he is even moderately enthusiastic about the way you came over, it is an encouraging sign.

You can learn from the professionals who come into your home. Television has helped to alter, and generally improve, the standard of public speaking. The public now expects to be addressed clearly, and in not too formal English, and to be entertained as well as informed.

Experience will help you to become an easy and confident speaker, and there are many victims you can practise on.

Guilds, men's clubs and other organisations are chronically short of fresh speakers.

If you have no subject which you feel compelled to speak on, in season and out of season, then approach the local road safety committee, the accident prevention authority, the National Savings organisers, your favourite political party. They will flood you with information and suggestions and will welcome with open arms another voice in their campaigns to educate the Great British Public.

Choose a subject near your own heart if you can.

But if I may choose one for you, what about the Blood Transfusion Service? Most areas of Britain are running with under-stocked blood banks (and this is one bank on which you cannot have an overdraft). If you can go and speak to outside bodies, stressing the fine work of the service, you will gain experience of speaking in public—but this will be a bonus on top of the real reward of the satisfaction of persuading your listeners to go along and give that life-saving gift.

A debating society can also be a good exercise ground. Debating is fun, and a real competitive sport—sometimes painfully close to a blood-sport when you get experienced and well-matched competitors.

Even without this extra practice, this book may prevent you from becoming like Lord Charles Beresford, of whom Sir Winston Churchill said, cuttingly, "He can best be described as one of those orators who, before they get up, do not know what they are going to say; when they are speaking, do not know what they are saying; and when they have sat down, do not know what they have said."

Charles Dickens, advising his son Harry before he made his first speech to Cambridge University Union, summed it all up—"Take any amount of pains about it (in preparation). Open your mouth well and roundly. Speak to the last person visible. And give yourself plenty of time."

The idea of the "strong silent man" and the "plain bloont man" has caused audiences a great deal of unnecessary suffering. A speaker who can get up on a platform and

"Debating is . . . a competitive sport . . ."

express his thoughts clearly is not necessarily an empty-headed patter-merchant. In defence of patter-merchants—few of them are as dull as your plain bloont man, and most come out with as big a proportion of sense.

Really good public speaking is a much more basic matter than having a typescript, a pleasant voice and a well-fitting suit. The best speakers are *alive*, on and off the platform. On the platform they show they are interested in their own subject and in what they have to say next. Off the platform, they are interested in other people; if you listen closely you can hear the pumps drawing in their conversation. They are the kind of people who do not have to be prodded with a sharp stick from time to time, just to check that they are still alive.

If you are not interested in your subject, how can you expect the audience out there in the Woodyard to be interested? The first, and sometimes most difficult, person to sell on the idea of a speech is yourself.

But you, remember, are unique.

There will Never be Another You

When anyone says "Why should people listen to me speaking? I'm nobody special," I reply with calculated rudeness, "Look, God in His wisdom and compassion made me as I am. God for His own dark purposes made you as you are. We are both unique. Hundreds of generations of differing ancestry and millions of minutes of differing personal experience have made us completely different.

"You may not be much, but you're all you've got—and there will never be another you!"

You are unique, so why serve up in your speeches, undigested, other folk's facts, ideas, reminiscences and opinions?

You are unique, so why lament that other people have qualities you know you do not possess? There is one glory of the sun and another glory of the moon. Some people can make bright witty after-dinner speeches, others are at their best putting over serious closely-argued economics.

In a universe so gloriously varied as to include the elephant and the flea, the whale, the duckbilled platypus and the praying mantis, there is surely room for your own particular kind of public speaking as well as your neighbour's.

Make the best of your raw material, and the fact that your speeches are different from others will be a matter for pride and enjoyment, not regret. And you can learn from others without being tempted to imitate them slavishly.

By being yourself, you can let your own natural style develop. Roger Ascham, tutor to Queen Elizabeth of England, said "Good style in England knows no tricks. To achieve simplicity and directness, let the style grow out of the subject."

For the sake of your own peace of mind and good opinion,

never trim your beliefs to suit your audience. Obviously, you will do your best to make a speech suit the occasion (what might please a rugby club stag-party might not suit the guests at a dinner after a funeral).

But be true to yourself. If you are a Tory do not pretend to Socialist sympathies when speaking in Left-wing company.

If you are a Christian, why set out to give the impression of being a swinging founder-member of the Permissive Society?

If you stand upon a public platform and pretend to be what you are not, you will be nervous and ill at ease. What is more, you will deserve to be. Be yourself—you will find it easier to live with yourself afterwards.

Mugwumps are rarely interesting as speakers. A mugwump, you remember, is an American magnate who sits on the political fence with his mug on one side and his wump on the other.

A speech-making mugwump produces carefully balanced arguments, but his "On the one hand . . ." and "On the other hand . . ." seldom add up to an exciting or even an interesting speech.

What a pleasure it is, in contrast, to listen to someone whose opinions are well-defined.

I come across people who feel that they are barred from speaking in public because they have not enough formal education. You can have the highest educational qualifications and still not be able to speak lucidly. You can lack them and still be able to move an audience.

I can think, for example, of a local politician with little formal education but with a great gift for public speaking. Listening to him, I would say to myself time and again "Oh no, not the barefoot bairns in the streets!" yet by the time he was well launched on the speech I would be sniffing into my handkerchief with the rest. Though to describe him as "the failed owner of a wee sweet-shop" would have been accurate, he was so much more than that, and, lacking formal education, he made full use of the abilities he had.

Others are deterred from speaking in public because they know they have a strong regional accent, nothing like the polished BBC tongue.

History shows that a strong accent, as long as it is not unintelligible, is not a bar to effective public speaking. Think of two extreme examples, Hitler and Napoleon!

The first had a strong provincial Austrian accent, the second was just as blatantly an Italian Corsican. If they could turn Europe upside down, maybe you could do something less ambitious but more laudible though your tongue betrays your origin every time you speak.

But slurred and sloppy English is something else again! You want to be understood, or you would not be speaking at all, so do not let chewed words and slovenly pronunciation get in the way. The English language deserves better than that!

If it fits in with your natural style, you can deliberately use a reputation for being big-headed to amuse an audience. Once, invited to speak at a Rotary Club by a member who had this reputation, I began by saying how pleased I was to be invited by Dave Cochrane.

"He and I share the same middle name. He is Dave Modesty Cochrane and I am Duncan Modesty Gillespie."

I let this sink in for a moment, while the members looked amused but puzzled. Then I added, "Of course, neither of us uses our middle name!"

If you have the kind of personality that will allow you to build up the image of "I know I'm big-headed, you know I'm big-headed, and we are all having a laugh at the fact" you can take the audience with you in the more important and serious parts of the speech.

But here again it is a matter for each speaker. A speaker whose modesty was almost painfully obvious would fall flat on his face if he tried to get away with this deliberate bombast. So, too, would a quietly conceited speaker. . . .

Tell a man he has no sense of humour and he is as hurt as if you had cast doubts on his virility or his driving ability. Yet the fact is that there are few more depressing sights than a speaker telling joke after joke in a vain effort to be funny—because he feels it is the duty of every public speaker to be funny.

You may never believe it if someone tells you that you have no sense of humour, but if you have tried repeatedly to tell jokes and light-hearted anecdotes and have failed, at least believe that you just do not have the ability to put across that kind of material.

Do not despair.

You are breaking no law by giving a serious (not a dull) speech, and your audience will enjoy it more than watching you floundering through a series of unfunny stories.

Capitalise on your assets. One of the most unusual speakers I ever listened to was a man called Andrew Spence. He would hold a sheaf of notes in his right hand, and when quoting detailed figures would glance down at them from time to time as if to refresh his memory.

Then he would turn a page, glance down, and carry on with his speech.

Everybody does that?

Yes, but Andrew Spence was stone blind.

He could not see the notes to which he referred, and his audience knew this—but by giving this appearance of normality he kept the listener's attention on his subject instead of on his great feat of memory.

He had all those figures in his *mind*, but he gave the impression that he had them at his *fingertips*.

Every speaker has his own natural pace.

Some seem to drawl in a friendly and leisurely way, like John Arlott and Ralph Whiteman; others let loose a cataract of words and yet remain perfectly clear.

Many years ago I reported the election campaign of a man with the latter ability; A. J. F. MacDonald stumped the constituency (successfully) for the Liberal Party, making several speeches a night at a pace of close on 220 words a minute. I met only one man who could take his speeches down verbatim, an Army officer who held his pencil poised vertically, while a rapid stream of tiny perfect shorthand characters flowed from its tip.

It did not matter that I could not record Mr. MacDonald's words verbatim. By the end of a few nights I could have stood up there and made the speeches for him, though at a mere hundred and forty words a minute.

Many libraries have collections of speeches—Crowned

Treasuries of Golden Oratory and the like—but to open them at random is to find how times have changed.

Some of those changes have been wrought by radio, reinforced by television. A speaker who affected those rounded periods and highflown attitudes would now be laughed off the platform, because radio and television have made us so familiar with a low-pitched almost conversational style of public speaking.

The generations before us, who could not take their drama from Peyton Place and Coronation Street, could find it in the hellfire sermons of the great divines, or the political speeches of giants like Charles Stewart Parnell, Gladstone, Lloyd George and the like.

But here again the unique nature of each speaker must be stressed.

I can think of one man, a small shopkeeper, who could only make one of those old-fashioned "ham" speeches and sound sincere—because it was his own style; put him on a platform and expect him to speak without orating, and then he would sound insincere.

"Take what you want and pay for it, says God." That Spanish proverb certainly applies to speaking, just as it does elsewhere in life.

If you are by nature a homely folksy kind of person and you work hard and become a Golden-Tongued Orator, a political demagogue, you will find that part of the price is that you become that kind of speaker and that kind of person.

The price on the ticket can be too high.

"Do your own thing" is a current catch-phrase which may be out of vogue though not out of date before you read this—it conveys a valuable idea.

Once I was speaking at a supper, and was very impressed by a solid well-prepared serious speech made by another man on the programme; at the end, I hurried to congratulate him and I was met by him half-way, as he came to congratulate me!

Yet the two speeches were very different. We had apparently both succeeded by "doing our own thing", and had not tried to make the other's type of speech.

Friends in the Woodyard

The first step to overcome the natural nervousness that you feel before making a speech is to remind yourself that the people out there in those endless rows of seats—the Woodyard—are your friends.

The audience is not a many-headed hostile animal waiting to pounce if you make the slightest mistake. It is a gathering of fellow-humans who wish you well, not only for your sake but for theirs.

Out of fellow-feeling and kindliness they hope you will do well. Out of understandable self-interest they hope that you will be bright, informative, original if possible, and not too lengthy.

In that endless time before the chairman introduces you, have a long look at the audience. Honestly, are they as formidable as all that?

Get it out of your head that you are their victim. The boot is on the other foot. For the next ten minutes, twenty minutes, or hour, they are your captives.

Be considerate to your captives. Give them, to the best of your ability, the kind of speech you would hope for if you were sitting on one of those hard seats down in the body of the hall.

You know that you are rather nervous and unsure of yourself, that you have an unpaid gas bill in one pocket, a really awkward letter in another, and a hole in your right shoe.

They don't know that.

Far crows, as they say, have fine feathers—and you are a "far crow" to your audience. In their eyes, if you were not a good speaker and an expert on your subject, you would not be there. . . .

Then, when you get to your feet, what do you think the members of the audience are thinking about? You?

Yes, but only in relation to themselves. "Am I going to be amused?" "Am I going to learn anything new from this chap about treacle-mining in the North of England?" "Am I going to be kept so late that I'll miss the last bus to the end of my road?"

For a speaker to be painfully self-conscious is in a real way to be self-centred and even selfish. It is the folk out there in the Woodyard who need your consideration. They are your prisoners.

One day I was sitting in a pub, which is not unusual. Less usually, I was sitting silent and listening, while for half an hour an acquaintance across the table told us in detail about a fishing trip.

Though I would never be unkind enough to remind him that, to me, fishing is summed up by the immortal words "A fly at one end and a fool at the other", he knows that angling is just not my subject. Yet, for all that time, he held the company's attention while he spoke, and I was as interested as anyone.

A day or two later I was at a function at which the angler was to propose the vote of thanks.

In the pub, his sentences had flowed from him. He must have uttered something like four thousand words. Now, with only a couple of hundred words to say, he was tongue-tied. He stuttered and stammered, went back on his tracks, and was most embarrassed.

Why?

The company was not much larger. The room was no more of a public place than the pub lounge had been.

His speech was poor not because of any shortcomings in his brain or his voice, but because his nerve failed him. Those who have done no public speaking cannot be blamed for saying "And I would have been the same!"

But why?

The people round the pub table were his friends, but the people at the presentation were in his mind an Audience—this many-headed beast which he had to placate as quickly as possible.

It is worth hammering home the point, again and again. The people out there in the Woodyard are your friends. They want you to make a good speech. They are as much your friends as the folk to whom you speak fluently in the office, or in the street, or at home, or, like the angler, round a table in the pub lounge.

If, while you are finding your feet as a speaker, you can arrange to speak on the subject that interests you most, it gives a great boost to your confidence.

And remember that "nerves" show less than you think. Not long ago a friend of mine had to make an important speech. I gave him what advice I could beforehand, and on the Great Day watched him closely as he spoke.

I was amazed at his calmness and confidence, the way he mustered his thoughts, paused when he had to pause, was unconcerned by any small slip of the tongue, but corrected himself and went on.

When he had finished he left the platform and went into the ante-room. I breezed in. "You spoke like a veteran," I said. "One of the best speeches I have heard in ages."

He did not heed me.

He was sitting shaking, white-faced, with the tears running

down his cheeks. "Oh God! Never again! Never again!" he kept muttering.

No amount of cajoling would make him believe that day that the nervousness which had been gnawing at him while he spoke was invisible even to those of us in the audience who were looking out for it. Later, after he had heard time and again what a fine speech he had made, he came to believe it a little—and went on to become an easy and confident speaker.

You may say "That's all very fine if I have time to prepare a speech. I am confident then. But what if I have a speech

. . . . on thin ice

sprung on me . . . ?"

If you are called on at short notice to speak, and have not had a chance to do your homework, keep in your mind's eye the image of a skater on thin ice.

He is skating along, and is suddenly aware that the ice had thinned under him. Does he slow down and falter? If he does, he finds himself up to the neck in broken ice and chilly water. Instead, he keeps up his pace, and his skates go singing over the thin patch—he has gone before the ice can break under him and let him down.

When you have thin material and a speech to make, do your best to emulate the expert skater and keep up the pace. You have only to think of some of the most successful comedians to realise that pace and confidence can make nondescript material seem sparkling.

"Keep up the pace" does not mean that you are to gabble along at a great rate. It means that you are not to hang around at the end of each sentence, that you are not to wait for applause, that you tell stories as if you enjoyed them and confidently expected your audience to do the same and that (maybe on the principle that a moving target is harder to hit) you avoid awkward pauses and long silences.

In the course of listening to thousands of speakers I have often heard passable material spoiled because the pace was slow and laboured; more rarely I have heard someone stand up and, with pace and confidence, spin out thin material until, like the fragile material of a soap-bubble, it glistened and shone.

"But this ability to skate over thin ice comes with experience!" you may say.

I wish it did. Some worthy people never learn the knack, perhaps because they have never known that the possibility existed.

Impromptu speaking can be made less frightening by reminding yourself that not a waking hour goes past but that you speak impromptu. Imagine that you and three or four friends are engaged in brisk conversation about business or about the fortunes of your favourite team. In the course of an hour you will make, impromptu, enough short speeches to fill seven or eight pages of this book.

Nothing you said might be so brilliant as to deserve to be recorded for posterity, yet it would be clearly uttered and lucidly expressed.

Impromptu speaking is like conversation, then . . . only more so.

Sometimes, after speaking impromptu, you sit down wondering where the flow of language has come from. The sentences seemed to spring fully-shaped to your mind as you needed them, complete with appropriate word-pictures and occasional light-hearted flashes.

I know of no way in which you can deliberately tap this flow of inspiration, but I do know that it comes most often when you are speaking about a subject on which you have strong feelings, either of enthusiasm or dislike. And, once again, the more you practise speaking without full notes, the easier it becomes.

On the other side of the coin—there are days when even brilliant impromptu speakers find the words dragging themselves to the front of their minds with the reluctance of mice running through golden syrup. Sometimes a very small amount of alcohol is enough to release that mental blockage

and start your thoughts flowing briskly—but when you are up there and speaking, it is too late to order a rum and Coca-Cola.

One way in which you can overcome the problem of nervousness and sharpen your impromptu speaking is to allow yourself to be recruited for Brains Trusts and Matters of Opinion. Almost every organisation, from political parties to Women's Guilds, have at some time or another to cast around to find speakers for a panel.

You may think that you will have no chance of preparing your material, since you will be speaking "off the cuff" in answer to questions you have never heard before, but this is not the case.

Some subjects crop up again and again; you are sure to be asked, on a general programme, about women's fashions, capital and corporal punishment and whatever news made the headlines that morning.

The art of working this prepared material into a discussion on a panel is to make it seem completely natural. To carry the thing to absurdity, what could look worse than to say "Now that question reminds me of an interesting experience I had in Kamchatka" and pull out a sheaf of notes, and read the story from them. . . .

Your primary role in a Brains Trust or Matter of Opinion team is to entertain the audience; if they are educated and informed as well, so much the better.

The first time you appear on a panel can be an ordeal. Then you discover that the spotlight is not on you all the time—it is shared by your fellow members. When you give a speech, you are under the spotlight all the time you are speaking; on a panel, you are not expected to speak for more than a quarter of the time, and if your fellow panellists like the limelight they will not be critical if you allow them more than their share.

You can say much or little on any topic, you can ride your hobby-horses when the questions suit you. An excellent training-ground for impromptu speaking.

Then, when you have appeared on several panels, you will start to perk up when you recognise old friends among the questions. With luck, only one or two of the audience will remember what you said last time, and this time, because of that little extra practice, you can make it sound so much better—and so much more spontaneous.

Most speakers benefit greatly from appearing on panels; it puts a sharper edge on their impromptu speaking. But it is a sad fact that there are some speakers, otherwise excellent on a platform, who fall to bits like a squashed biscuit when faced with the chance of answering spontaneous questions in public.

Others (and they are less easy to discourage) give five-minute speeches whether they have anything to say or not.

Sometimes a speaker like that can at least give someone else an opening. I have happy memories of a member of a panel who rather solemnly told us of his experiences on the Amazon, where a tribe had given up drug-taking when they started playing football.

"They did it for kicks?" I suggested.

Another confidence-builder. Branches of Toastmasters International can be found in many of the principal British cities and towns.

The movement was based on Santa Ana, California, and was founded by an American, Ralph C. Smedley. You will find in the movement the pseudo-religious zeal that seems common to many American enterprises, and this may not be to your taste, but there is no doubt in my mind, as an ex-member, of the usefulness of the Toastmasters in giving new speakers confidence and every chance to exercise their abilities.

The new member goes through a Basic Training programme based on a series of twelve speeches, beginning with his Ice-breaker on a subject he knows well, like his own job or his background.

He goes on to one in which he is invited to "Be in Earnest" and speak on a subject on which he has definite convictions. And, as he goes on to others, he learns more about building a speech, about the use of gestures and of visual aids, and vocal variety.

Each speech is assessed and commented upon by an evaluator, a fellow-member. Warning lights, each time a Toastmaster speaks, remind him when he approaches or passes the nominated time for the address.

. . . . *anything to say or not.*

Members also gain experience in chairmanship as Toastmaster of the evening, taking over the running of the entire programme.

"Table Topics", which allow every member to participate in debate or to speak impromptu and briefly on a theme, are a feature of each session.

If there is a local branch of the Toastmasters, membership may be a great help to you even if you remain a member only for a year or two. Then looking back you may, like me, be heartily glad you joined—and heartily glad that you are no longer a member.

The dreadful earnestness of some of the members put me off!

As a young man, entering for public speaking contests was one of the ways I hammered the "nerves" out of my system.

I would wait, keyed up, for the moment when I would be summoned on to the platform, and a voice within me would say: "Go up there! Shake them with the originality of your thought, impress them with the clarity of your delivery, thrill them with your attack on their emotions, interest them with . . ." and then another wee nervous voice inside me would interrupt with "Who? Me?"

So I never did achieve those heights, though I reached the prize-list from time to time—but I found out early that the best cure for nerves is to get up there and speak.

It was, looking back, a cruel training. The subjects were sprung on you ten minutes before the "off". "Permanent pastures versus temporary leys" was one which is burned on my mind. I was lumbered with that at a Young Farmers' Club contest—and I was not a farmer. But, knowing that I had to speak for ten minutes or stand silent till the time was up, I spoke!

Do not be too discouraged if you have already spoken half a dozen times in public and feel that you have died the death. The chances are that you did much better than you feared—and anyway, if you did fail, you are in excellent company. It is not the end of the road. It is the beginning.

Dale Carnegie, whose books still sell by the million though he has been dead for years, taught thousands of people to be effective public speakers—yet he failed miserably the first half dozen times he tried to speak in public.

And they called Lloyd George the Welsh Wizard, because he was a spell-binding speaker as well as being a British Prime Minister (they are not always the same thing, as you may have noticed). They called a raspberry after him, because he was so good at raising Cain. But he once confessed that the first time he attempted to make a public speech he was in a state of misery.

"It is no figure of speech, but literally true, that my tongue clove to the roof of my mouth, and at first I could hardly get out a word."

The more public speaking you do, the easier it is to control your nerves. You may never lose that "Over the top and into action" feeling as you are called on to rise and speak, but the worst of the collywobbles are forgotten.

This is no great consolation to a raw speaker. It's like telling a girl who is troubled by blushing "You'll grow out of it as you grow older." She does not want to be free of that rosy glow in ten years' time—it is now she is concerned with.

"Are there no practical hints for conquering nervousness *now*?"

One very effective physical device has the nervous feeling literally leaking out of your fingertips.

As you rise to speak, clench your fists as tightly as possible, and draw in a deep breath and hold it. You will be disconcerted to find that you are suddenly more nervous.

But now let your hands slowly relax, and breathe slowly out.

It is like a miracle. You can feel your nervousness leave you, leaking out at the tips of those relaxed fingers.

It takes less time to do all this than to read the words; the audience will notice nothing unusual. But you will be heartened and encouraged by the change in your own feelings.

A miracle?

No, just an interesting example of the two-way traffic between mind and body. When you feel angry, you scowl . . . but if you deliberately scowl you begin to feel angry. When you are friendly to someone you smile pleasantly . . . but if you smile pleasantly at someone you find it much easier to feel friendly towards him.

In the same way, when you stand up there and deliberately relax, you trigger off all the mental and physical reactions which enable you to feel as relaxed as you look.

It worked for me. I cannot remember if someone taught me the "trick" or whether I invented it for myself. If the idea was devised by someone else, I am delighted to thank him publicly on behalf of myself and all the people who have been helped by this very simple and effective method of dispelling pre-speech nerves.

Once upon a time there was a minister who wanted to play golf on a Saturday afternoon when he should have been preparing his sermon. "God will speak to me in the pulpit," he said, as he brought out his golf-clubs. And, next morning, God did speak to him in the pulpit. He said, "Young man, you haven't prepared your sermon."

The minister was, naturally, nervous as he flannelled his way through the rest of the service.

One way to avoid unnecessary nervousness is to learn from the minister's bad example, and make sure you have prepared your subject as well as you can. You know what you want to say, to whom you want to say it, and how you intend to say it? That alone is enough to remove a great part of your nervousness.

It helps, too, if you enjoy your subject. A speaker who knows his subject, and enjoys what he knows, is more than half-way there and has no need to be nervous.

Everyone has his own enthusiasms. With some it's the early codices of the Bible; with others, it's bowling, or wine-making, or growing roses on heavy soils. Or treacle-mining through the ages.

If, up there and speaking on your favourite subject, you do "dry", do not let nervousness come flooding in.

Try a little "flannel".

Amplify what you have just said, introducing the extra material with "By the way" or "Before I leave that subject". With any luck, by the time you have flannelled your way through a further sentence or two, your mind will have snicked back into gear again and you will be able to go on from where you left off.

". . . why mind showing emotion?"

Confidence can come from knowing how to quit while you are still ahead.

You may be called on to make a serious speech, and find when you stand up that you are really beaten before you start. The audience may just have had a huge meal; they may be fidgetting on hard seats after a long afternoon of dull speeches; they may be sunk half-asleep in deep seats or half-cut after too many samples of wine; they may be restless because time is getting on and they are going to miss the last bus.

When you know that the odds are stacked against you, the kindest solution (both for you and your listeners) is to pare the serious part of your speech down to the bare minimum, leaven the lump with a story or two, and release the listeners well before they expect to be set free.

But be honest with yourself—be sure that you are not just making an excuse out of nervousness or laziness for trimming back your speech.

To gain confidence, keep accepting invitations. But try to avoid having to make a speech just before a meal. It takes a really great orator to compete with the attractions of fillet steak and fried onions. If you find yourself in this dilemma, do not try to get a long serious message across.

Two or three brief remarks, maybe an appropriate joke. . . .

What your audience is really waiting eagerly for is a little speech that begins "For what we are about to receive . . ."

Some people are nervous of speaking in case they show emotion. But, remembering that you are speaking to friends, why should you mind showing emotion—genuine emotion—during a speech?

Once, after a tour of Donegal as the guests of the Irish Tourist Board, I was recruited to propose a vote of thanks. I was humorous and eloquent—glib is perhaps the word—until I came to speak of the friends we had made on the brief tour and would perhaps never meet again. I choked up and had to sit down.

The applause was tremendous, but it was the kind of effect that no honest speaker could achieve on purpose.

Envious of a speaker who did not mind making a fool of himself, but jumped in and splashed around, I asked him for his secret. "I realised long ago than when they were laughing at me they were leaving someone else alone!"

A Look is a Light Touch

In books on public speaking you come across the phrase "Eye contact". What does it amount to? Looking at the people you are talking to, just as you would in conversation.

Not letting your eyes move from floor to ceiling without glancing at the faces in between. Not staring out over the people in the Woodyard with the unfocussed look that betrays the fact that you are not really looking at anything. No—really looking at the audience.

To begin with, you have to force yourself to look, because to meet someone's eyes is to make contact with them, almost as if you had reached out and touched them lightly.

It is, after all, no wonder that even in those allegedly civilised times we should be apprehensive of standing up and being faced with hundreds of staring eyes.

Desmond Morris, author of *The Naked Ape*, says that among primates (which includes human beings as well as monkeys and apes), "A direct stare is typical of the most out-and-out aggression.

"During ordinary face-to-face conversations we typically look away from our companions when we are talking, then glance back at them at the end of each sentence or "paragraph" to check their response to what we have said. A professional lecturer takes some time to train himself to look directly at the members of his audience instead of over their heads, down at his rostrum, or out towards the side or back of the hall.

"Even though he is in such a dominant position, there are so many of them, all staring (from the safety of their seats) at him, that he experiences a basic and initially uncontrollable fear of them.

"Only after a great deal of practice can he overcome this.

"The simple aggressive physical act of being stared at by a large group of people is also the cause of the fluttering 'butterflies' in the actor's stomach before he makes his entrance on to the stage.

"He has all his intellectual worries about the qualities of his performance and its reception, but the massed threat-stare is an additional and more fundamental hazard for him."

This reaction to the threat-stare dates back to the times when man's ancestors were not even recognisably human.

A long and interesting speech could be prepared about another fear of staring—perhaps it grew out of the "threat-stare".

People at all periods of history, and in all parts of the world, have believed in the Evil Eye—have believed that some individuals can bring misfortune, illness and even death to other human beings, animals and plants merely by looking at them.

Sometimes the individual knew he had this power, sometimes it was involuntary. One man bewitched his own cattle without meaning to, and the story goes that another unfortunate Yorkshireman always fixed his first glance of the morning on a pear-tree outside his house. The tree withered and died....

With hundreds of generations of superstitious ancestors behind us, it is no wonder that "establishing eye contact" is not as easy as some folk make out, and that like the Yorkshireman's pear tree we "wither and die" the first time we go on a platform and face the barrage of eyes.

But there is no need to wear blue beads, or amulets, or red thread with seven knots in it, or to fill the beaker on the speaker's table with water which has been drawn in a wooden ladle from a running stream and had gold or silver coins dropped in it.

The people out there are not ill-wishing us. The folk in the Woodyard are our friends, remember.

No Need to Fight or Flee

When you stand on a platform and nervousness makes your palms sweat and your heart race, a great many complex changes are taking place in your body. Adrenalin, for instance, is pumping into your blood-stream, and giving you the kind of boost that (if you had been like our ancestral man-ape in the Olduvai Gorge in Africa) would have carried you in a series of wild leaps up the cliff-face away from a charging leopard, or nerved you to turn and fight a menacing baboon-pack.

We can neither fight nor flee, but the adrenalin boost helps to nerve us to better efforts as speakers.

If you are a visiting speaker, and a stranger in a strange land, you can help to make matters easier by getting "the feel of the course". Even if you only wander into the hall in which you will be speaking, go up on the platform, and imagine the Woodyard of empty seats populated by eager listeners, it will help to take away some of the strangeness which everyone feels, however experienced, when they stand up in an unfamiliar hall and launch away.

If the hall is already filling up when you arrive you may not be able to do all this, but it is worth while having a discreet look, perhaps from the ante-room door or from the balcony, at the hall in which you will be speaking.

On the conscious level you know, as visiting speaker, that you are very welcome (the organisers have been sweating in case you failed to turn up), but at a deeper subconscious level you are a strange animal trespassing on the territory of others of your kind.

Anything you can do to familiarise yourself with the place in which you will be speaking helps to reassure that timid animal deep down in your subconscious that you are not going to be driven away with angry barks and growls.

Many people, especially those unused to vigorous physical exercise, breathe with only a small proportion of their lung capacity. Pearl-fishers and yogi experts can display tremendous powers of breath control, but the public speaker does not need to go as far as that.

All he has to do is consciously, and from time to time, to take long breaths of fresh air and hold them for a few moments before releasing them gently.

Breathe good fresh air for choice—but you may not be able to find it easily nowadays and will have to make do with the atmosphere you can get.

This simple exercise will pay dividends quickly. To go on to a public platform and know that you can easily hold enough breath to see you through the longest paragraph is a boost to your confidence.

If you allow yourself to become short of breath on-stage, you will find yourself feeling nervous. The nervousness will then make you feel flustered . . . and breathless.

It is far better to take an unscheduled deep breath in the middle of a sentence than to plough on to the last gasp, when you will feel that you should bend double for a moment to get rid of the vacuum which is imploding your lungs.

How can you avoid getting into this painful breathless predicament? Chiefly by avoiding nervous haste. Take it a little easier—you haven't a train to catch, and there is no trophy for rattling through a speech in record time.

Another cause of breathlessness is using too much wind for shouting. If you are faced with a big hall and no microphone, you are tempted to shout instead of speaking. This takes more breath.

You can speak loudly and clearly without shouting, by using the muscles across your diaphragm at waist-level for voice-production.

The British government paid me to develop mine, on a drill square in the north of Italy. Down one side of the square was a Fascist barracks; down the other side ran a canal bringing swift blue-grey snow water from the Dolomites. We were divided into two ranks, each soldier taking a turn to drill his opposite number in the other rank. You soon learned to develop those muscles so that your one-man platoon would hear the "Aye-Bout Turrrrn" and would not purposely walk straight into the canal.

When you have to "turn up the volume" you will soon know whether you are using those muscles—you will feel them tensing and forcing the words out.

Another way in which you can recruit your body to help your mind to overcome nervousness is by pulling yourself up straight, though without straining, while you are speaking. If you stand tall, you not only look confident, you feel more confident too.

An easy stance can help you to feel more at ease on the platform. Standing on the balls of both feet, with one foot slightly in front of the other, gives you the sensation of being on your toes without being on tiptoe. Keep clear of the furniture, though it is tempting towards the end of a long speech to lean lightly on the back of a chair.

I like the old-fashioned lectern to speak from; when I grow emphatic it gives me something to thump, though I cannot match the aged John Knox, who had to be helped up into the pulpit then preached so vigorously that he seemed likely to knock it into kindling-sticks.

The first time you make a speech your hands feel as big and awkward as road-maker's shovels. What do you do with them?

The Lapel-grasper solves the problem by taking a strangle-hold on his own lapels.

"Innocence Surprised in the Bath" clasps his hands in front of him.

When I start a speech, I usually have my note-cards in my left hand at chest height, and my right hand hanging at my side with my thumb hooked lightly in my trouser pocket. Once I warm to the work, I forget about my hands except to use them for emphasis. And I certainly do that.

I am not at all like the Prince Philip fan, who stands with his hands behind his back and feels no need to gesture or to shift his stance. I use gestures liberally (you could gag me by tying my hands behind my back) and make full use of the platform.

"You prowl back and forwards—you're a restless being!" I was told once. I suspect that this prowling looks quite natural when I do it, but that one of the static speakers who tried to prowl on purpose would look out of character and comical.

Even if you feel it difficult to use gestures and still feel natural, at least try to let your feelings and your meaning be mirrored in your expression. Unless you are a professional comedian using it as a gimmick, a deadpan expression is very disconcerting to your audience.

Bears get an undeserved bad name for treachery because they do not signal their feelings, and do not show their hostility by their facial expression in the way humans and tigers do—they still look like your old cuddly teddy bear while they are pulling you into raw chops.

Don't be like a bear, let the listeners see what you are feeling as well as hear what you are saying.

One gesture which helps you and helps your audience when appropriate is to tick off your points clearly on your fingers.

Try to keep to a maximum of five points (six if like Ann Boleyn you have six fingers on each hand). Once you get on to the second hand, what is otherwise helpful becomes complicated. By the time you reach "And tenth . . ." the patient people out there are glad that you were born with only the normal quota of fingers and that you show no signs of taking off your shoes and continuing the tally on your toes.

If you do use this gesture, and grip hold of each finger on your left hand in turn, do not leave too long between the points. The audience are sitting waiting for each point to arise—that is the purpose of the gesture. Besides, you do not look your most dignified standing for minutes at a time clasping your left forefinger.

A microphone—like gestures—can be a great help in getting your message across, but remember that it may be an invitation to mutter and that you may find that you come across less clearly than if you discard it and lift up your natural speaking voice.

Keep a uniform distance from the mike (not ostentatiously,

. . . . *tick off your points clearly on your fingers.*

you can move quite a bit between sentences) and this will save your voice from fluctuating unnaturally and disconcerting your listeners.

The public speaker, experienced or novice, has his share of pests to deal with. There is the shatterer, the interrupter, the hostile heckler, the earnest inquirer, the crank, the planted questioner, and many more.

There is no fixed way of dealing with them.

The chatterers, who are the commonest distraction are best dealt with by standing silent and looking at them until they get the message and shut up—but I admit that that takes a good deal of confidence.

As for the others, the one golden rule is not to lose your temper. While you keep your temper, and seem to be struggling to give fair play to people who are being unpleasant to you, you will hold the sympathy of the audience.

If a heckler gets home with a well-directed wisecrack, then laugh, even if it hurts.

I find the persistent earnest inquirer is the most difficult· The best remedy is to ask him to write out a list of questions and promise to see him afterwards.

Only rarely are you justified in being devastatingly rude to an interrupter. Remember the happy example of the speaker who had suffered blasts of a bugle until at last he smiled sweetly and said, "And what else did Mummy give you for your Christmas, sonny?"

The Mogambo Trap

Once upon a time a very young official went out to Africa. When he reached the remote area of which he was to be in charge, he summoned the chief and told him he was going to address his people.

All the tribe gathered in the middle of the village.

They listened while he told them of the Great White Queen over the water, whose heart was full of love for even the smallest piccaninny, and they raised their spears and shouted "Mogambo!"

They listened while he spoke of the Empire on which the sun never set—this was some years ago—and they raised their spears and shouted "Mogambo!"

They listened while he assured them that he would rule like a just and kindly father and that they could bring all their troubles to him—and again they lifted their spears and shouted "Mogambo".

At last the indaba was over, and the chief showed the young official round the village. As they passed the boma where the cattle were kept, the chief led him over to admire the tribe's best bulls, but he warned the young man "Watch your feet, bwana. The mogambo is very thick on the ground around the bull-ring!"

Public speakers should remember that story, for given the temptation it is very easy to slip head over heels into the Mogambo Trap.

Your audience may not raise their spears and shout "Mogambo!" but when you indulge in purple passages and high-flown oratory it isn't "Brilliant speaker!" they're murmuring.

It's "Mogambo!"

Audiences will put up with a great variety of faults in a speaker. They will sit through speeches which seem as endless and dry as a bicycle run across the Gobi Desert. They will tolerate a quiet speaker who can only be heard when he lifts his voice to a loud whisper near the mike. But they will become restive if they think they are being patronised.

There must be times when it is very difficult to avoid sounding patronising. If you are the Prime Minister addressing the lifers in Dartmoor . . . though even there, to be patronising and adopt the "from Me up here to you down there" attitude, would be bad manners.

Children are the worst sufferers from this. Think of almost any prize-giving ceremony. . . . But one hint of patronising, of speaking down to them, and you have lost a young audience. You may have to adjust your vocabulary a little, but otherwise talk to children as if they were small human beings. After all, most of them are.

Patronising is an easy trap to fall into with adults too—for example "Jim here", referring to Sir James Follenfant, K.B.E., the chairman you met for the first time ten minutes earlier. "You good folks down in this quiet little corner of Kent"—to them, that corner of Kent is the centre of the world.

One way to avoid the Mogambo Trap, and unnaturally high-flown language, is to ensure that the feeling that you express in your speeches is your own. Enthusiasm is generally infectious—but not always.

As a young schoolboy just learning geometry I was struck by the beauty of the orderly presentation of Euclid's proofs—the kind of order which, to my romantic mind, kept the stars in their courses.

I was called on to give a proof, and did so with some enthusiasm.

Half-way through, the maths teacher stopped me and said, sourly, "You're not reciting poetry now!" That killed my enthusiasm for geometry instantly. It did not kill my enthusiasm for the teacher—I had none.

Happily, you are unlikely as an adult to come across such ostentatious bad manners.

Part of good manners, on a speaker's part, is to approach the event professionally. You were keen when you agreed to come and speak, but you are less keen now; you have a hang-over, your rates are due, and your mother-in-law is coming to visit. You may be tempted to say "What the Hell!" and give something less than your best, but why should your poor captives in the Woodyard suffer from your slipshod and amateurish approach?

You may not be a professional speaker, in that there is no cheque waiting for you at the end of the evening, but your listeners are spending their time and giving their attention, and are entitled to your best.

If Harry Lauder could go on stage and do his act, though he had a telegram in his pocket telling him that his loved son had been killed in action, you surely can lay aside your hang-over, your overdue bills and your mother-in-law's visit, and give the best you've got.

That best is likely to get better if you can turn a cold clear eye on your own shortcomings. It is one thing to realise your own unique potentialities and quite another to be blind to your own faults.

If you find that your audiences drift into sleep after five minutes, it may be because your material is deadly dull—but it may also be because your voice ticks on with the monotonous regularity of a metronome, or because you are swinging back and forwards and literally hypnotising your listeners.

Whatever the reason, do not curse the audience—alter your faults.

Time and again I hear speakers complaining about the reaction of an audience. They don't applaud much. They sit there like bags of wet cement.

Paradoxically, it makes public speaking a good deal simpler when you realise that the people out there in the Woodyard do not owe you any duty at all.

No, that is not entirely true. They owe you the civility of sitting still, keeping quiet, and (if they fall asleep) not snoring loudly.

All the duty is on your side. . . .

I like food and drink in liberal but not (I hope) excessive

" . . . a real belt-tightener . . . "

quantities, but those two pleasures have their drawbacks for speakers. You go to a dinner well-prepared to speak, confident, interested in what you are going to say. You have a meal that is everything that you could wish, but by the time the empty Peach Melba dishes have been cleared away, and the biscuits coffee and cheese set down, you are in a mood of happy somnolence, and the sharp cutting edge has gone off your enthusiasm.

There is no reason why you should sit and push the good food around your plate, but it is unwise to tuck into a real belt-tightener when you are on the speech-list.

Drink?

For some years, the only time I drank rum was just before I made a speech. Maybe subconsciously I equated it with the tot of rum soldiers used to be served with just before they went "over the top" in the trenches. I used to think it helped the flow of my speech, but now I am not so sure.

Whether a moderate amount of drink is helpful to you, or hinders you, is something you must find out for yourself. Certainly, err on the side of moderation, unlike the young and nervous minister.

He was preaching in a strange church, and the kindly beadle told him that the parish minister often had a drop of whisky to steady his nerve. Offering the young man a half-bottle of whisky, the church officer was appalled to see the contents disappear in a couple of swigs.

The young minister preached like a man possessed. He thumped the bookboard, he lifted his congregation heavenwards or swung them trembling out over the smoking pit of Hell. When he was being unrobed in the vestry after the service he asked the beadle how he had done.

"Fine, minister, fine," he said, and added the supreme Scottish compliment "I've heard worse many a time." Then he added quietly, "But David slew Goliath with a pebble from the brook. He didn't take his catapult and knock the big ——'s head in!"

Eat sparingly, lest the bulk of the food and the effort of digestion clog your mind; and drink sparingly, lest the alcohol has too much of the opposite effect and you find yourself saying brilliantly words which in the morning you wish you had left unsaid.

It was the Best Butter

Remember the scene in Alice in Wonderland in which the Mad March Hare has some trouble with his watch and finds that the application of butter has done more harm than good? "It was the best butter," he says, meekly. But it still did not work.

Listening to a particularly overdone speech, I find myself murmuring "It was the best butter!"

Butter in speeches, as on bread, should not be applied too liberally, but there are times when it is appropriate.

Old John, on the verge of tears, is retiring after fifty-four years with the firm. This is no time to recall that he was an ill-tempered boy when he came in the Old King's time, that he matured into an ill-tempered man, and that now even his best friend would have to admit that he is a cantankerous old devil.

There are ways of getting round all that.

You remember that he sat and glowered at everyone who arrived later than himself in the morning, and you say, perfectly truthfully, "His time-keeping has been a lesson to us all."

And you can always fall back on the truthful but vague "The place just won't be the same without old John." You need not add that it will be a relief to go past his corner without wondering whether he will come snapping out at you, like a weasel out of a drystone wall, with some real or imagined grievance.

The best butter, after all, is pleasant in texture—not oily.

To praise someone for a quality you know he does not possess, he knows he does not possess, and the audience knows he does not possess, is not "butter" but flattery, and flattery of the worst kind—the kind that is not only insincere but obviously insincere.

You spread butter with a knife, not with a trowel.

One of the commonest pats of butter is to say when introducing a speaker, "Mr. Cartwright, who needs no introduction to this audience . . ." and then to introduce him in great detail.

"Who needs no introduction" is one of those "Some phrases seldom ring true" expressions we all use; it pleases the person you are introducing, and does no-one else any harm. But you can make it ring true by drawing attention to it.

"It is often said of visiting speakers that they need no introduction, but in the case of Mr. Cartwright who is known to all of us as an acknowledged local expert on treacle-mining, this is literally true. Mr. Cartwright, who needs no introduction to *this* audience, is going to tell us about a recent significant discovery in the treacle-bearing strata of the Yorkshire Lower Cambrian measures. Mr. Cartwright!"

If you use too much butter in introducing a speaker it can be very embarrassing for him. I remember once being introduced by a chairman who laid on the butter with a generous hand.

I was the most polished and humorous speaker they had ever heard. I was a fund of originality, the deviser of innumerable jokes, and so on, and so on.

It wasn't true. Not all of it. . . .

I stood up with a sinking feeling; how could I ever live up to that introduction?

So I stood and looked at the audience for thirty seconds or so, while they stared back at me.

"Do you know what you remind me of? Row after row of tombstones. You're sitting there thinking 'Go on, make me laugh!' And I don't blame you!"

At that, they relaxed and laughed, and the harm done by the excess butter was partly undone.

Some speeches fall into the "friendly noise" class. They are not intended to convey any information, nor to educate or excite the audience. I suppose they could be as effectively given in Amharic, Urdu or Gibberish. They assure the listeners of the speaker's goodwill.

In a "friendly noise" speech (for example the brief remarks made at a dinner by a representative of one of the guest organisations) a fair amount of the best butter is not only excusable—it is expected.

Also in the category of "Some phrases seldom ring true"—"*With your permission* I shall now turn to consider the history of the Ottoman Empire in the following century," or "*Perhaps you will permit me to say* . . ." or "*If you don't mind*, we will pass over the subject of. . . ."

While you are on your feet and speaking, you are the boss, and the fact that those phrases are an empty formality is easily demonstrated. When you say "With your permission . . " do you really expect anyone to stand up in the Woodyard and shout "I refuse permission. Leave that subject till some other day!"

You can tactfully convey information to your audience with a pat of butter by "reminding" them of facts which perhaps they never knew.

"You remember how, in the spring of last year, the Prime Minister in a letter to the Treacle-Miner's Union, made a strong case for . . ."

This is a very useful device, as long as you do not fall into the trap of reminding listeners of something of which it is very unlikely that they have ever heard. Like the parish minister who said in his sermon to a sleepy summer Sunday congregation, "You will well remember how Lucretius wrote 'Tantum religio potuit suadere malorum'."

In argumentative debate, you can put the butter-dish right to the back of your mental cupboard, and get stuck in enthusiastically; Admiral William F. Halsey's formula for waging war was "Hit hard, hit fast, hit often" and it is a good motto in this kind of disputation. And it is great fun, and great practice!

I have relished it not only in public halls, but in public houses, and even on a stretch of waste ground in the middle of a miners' village in the small hours of the morning.

Disputation used to be a Scottish hobby—the Scots rarely fell into the mistaken belief, like some Englishmen, that noisy argument is bad manners or intended to be hurtful. But television, I fear, has helped to kill this as well as other participating sports.

Five hundred years ago and more, the Scots poets used to have "flyting matches". They would choose an opponent,

" . . . *no hard feelings* . . . "

and blackguard him with every epithet they could lay their pens to, in verse.

Knowing the rules, and taking the abuse in the spirit in which it was meant, the opponent would reply, miscalling his attacker in turn, in verse.

Both knew that this was done in sport, and the abuse generally left no hard feelings behind.

In the same way, if you have a friend who is a confident speaker, you can arrange a "no holds barred" debate as an entertainment. It is the verbal equivalent of all-in wrestling, and has to be set up carefully—it is important to do no serious damage in the ring, and to leave it good friends.

Some speakers, even the most famous and distinguished among them, never learn one elementary branch of platform manners—consideration for other speakers.

All right, you have made your speech and anything that follows is bound to be an anti-climax. But that does not mean that you should sit fidgetting on the platform while others are speaking, or that you should glance ostentatiously at your watch—or shake it to see if it has stopped. Or yawn behind your hand.

Or you are the last speaker? You know and I know that the best must be to come, but listen to the others with the good manners you would expect from them. Do nothing to distract them, or the audience.

It is tempting, when you are further down the programme, to take out your notes and bone up on them while you have the chance (even Abraham Lincoln fell into that trap), but don't do it.

Sit quietly in your place, and give as good an impression of interest as you can muster.

Anyone who has a ready gift of words finds himself tempted from time to time to flay his opponents with whips and scorpions. Leave the whips and scorpions at home. "Knocking copy" is avoided by advertisers, who have to know all the tricks because they lose money if they do not, and "knocking copy" is better avoided in speeches too.

An all-out attack on an opponent may be enjoyed by your hearers at the time, but somehow, illogically, some of the mud you have skilfully flung at the other person sticks to you.

Remember instead the example of the golfer who was giving a stroke-by-stroke account of a game. "That man's putting! Dead-on!" he said enthusiastically. "And I never came across a player as skilful at getting his ball out of a rough lie! And you'll hardly credit it, but he drove the second in one, right on to the green!"

"And how much did he beat you by?" his friend asked sympathetically

"Beat me? I beat him!"

The very opposite of knocking copy, but the speaker came out of it with an enhanced reputation.

In the same way, instead of saying "Mr. Cartwright's

ignorance of treacle-mining in Peru is only matched by his impudence in expressing an opinion at all!", you can say "Mr. Cartwright, whose knowledge of treacle-mining in Yorkshire is beyond doubt, has been led astray by his own specialised knowledge when he speaks of treacle-mining in Peru. He has not taken into account the fact that because of the big difference in temperature, treacle in Peru is lower in viscosity, and . . ."

You can certainly cut someone down to size without resorting to outright abuse.

There used to be a local football team whose supporters were famous for their dislike of referees. While the home team was winning, the barrage of abuse was restrained, but let the team drop a goal behind and the noise rose to a crescendo.

And on this Saturday afternoon the home team were five goals down. . . . It was a nasty cold, wet day, and the crowd warmed themselves by venting their feelings.

Then came a disputed penalty.

For five minutes the hills behind the pitch rang with yells, screams and oaths, but the referee stood smiling and unshaken while his parentage back to the days of Robert the Bruce was dissected and found wanting.

At last, through sheer lack of breath, the fans fell silent.

Out of that silence came a small sweet voice. "Oh, you silly, silly little referee!"

And the referee winced. Though so mild, it was the only criticism that got home to him.

In the same way, from the platform, you can say, "I am very disappointed that someone for whose opinion I have so much respect, and who in his past speeches has agreed with me on this important subject, should now . . . mistakenly, I am quite certain . . . have abandoned his previous views." It is much more effective than mouthfuls of invective.

It was the best butter. . . .

The Harvest of Facts

"There is no expedient to which a man will not resort to avoid the real labour of thinking,' said Sir Joshua Reynolds, the famous painter—and to prepare a good speech takes some of that real labour. Where do the necessary ideas and facts come from?

I tend to find the time I spend shaving particularly productive of ideas. As the blade glides over my cheeks I let my mind wander round the subject, and it is unusual if I do not come up with some new facet or some striking turn of phrase. And while I shave in the bathroom there is always something available to jot a new idea down on.

Do not think you will remember that bright idea. You will not. Note it down at once on the back of an envelope, a paper bag, a cigarette packet, then transfer the note to something more permanent and tidy when you have time.

When I have a beard, I find I lose this daily minute or two for reflection. But there are other times and other places, and if you let your mind wander constructively you will find that you have the basic ideas for a number of speeches—good speeches at that.

You can slide into a deep hot bath worrying about a speech, and come out after a long relaxing steep with no worries but with plenty of good ideas. The fact that you will also have a schoolgirl complexion all over is a happy bonus.

And some people think best with their feet. They walk and walk, paying little heed to the scenery but pausing in mid-stride from time to time to take a note. If they do not move their lips too obviously in silent speech or gesture too

ostentatiously, no-one notices that the walker is really a thinker.

When ideas fail to come, try dredging down into your subconscious by letting your imagination run free. One way of doing this is by word association. Write down the subject of your speech, "Treacle-mining in Yorkshire", or whatever it may be, then immediately under this write the first word that comes into your head. It might be "moors". Next one "curlews" . . . and already you have a theme for part of your speech—"Treacle-mining and its effect on the wild life of hitherto unspoiled countryside."

Sometimes you can achieve the same result by sitting back in a comfortable chair and letting your mind wander without troubling to note the "clues". But do not expect people to believe that you are working hard. They will think that you are doing nothing, or even napping. For some reason, in this bustling society you may waste all the time you please looking at a picture on the goggle-box, but to sit back and enjoy the pictures on your own television screen is suspect. . . .

After the preliminary skirmishing, you have to decide what you want the speech to achieve.

Do you want it to make the audience take out their wallets and support a good cause? Or to make converts to your point of view? or, perfectly reasonably, to say "What an amusing after-dinner speaker that chap is!"

When you have the intention of the speech clear in your mind you can start to arrange the material in it.

Having a skeleton helps. When the speech is complete this framework should not be noticeable but, like Miss Universe, a speech without a skeleton is shapeless.

When you start to jot down the speech, help yourself and your potential audience by building into the first few sentences a clear statement of what the speech is about.

This can be done in a direct way—"I propose in the next ten minutes to remind you of some of the problems facing the treacle-mining industry in Yorkshire today" and this can be reinforced later in the speech by such sentences as "You will see, then, that Yorkshire treacle-miners have their problems, not all of their own making."

Or it can be done in various ways indirectly. The direct way has much to commend it, for the danger of indirect references is that the audience may miss the point and fail to appreciate just why you were up there and speaking at all.

So when you are preparing material for a speech, remember the "to" clause. You are not just going to make a speech—you are going to make a speech to please, to interest, to amuse, to persuade, to infuriate.

Yes, to infurate! There is great satisfaction in getting up in front of an audience completely hostile to you and your ideas, and hammer away at them with the ironical message "No doubt but ye are the people and wisdom shall die with you."

Whatever the purpose, it is worth going to a great deal of trouble to choose your material and shape it to suit the particular audience you have in view. As Lloyd George used to say, you bait the hook to catch the fish.

When I am researching for a material for a book, a speech or an article, I have a personal motto—"Just one book more!" It is in my experience in the last and least likely book that you come up with some fact or quotation that will illuminate the whole subject.

You may end with substantially more material than you will ever be able to weave into one speech, but that does not matter; in a mysterious way, the knowledge you have but do not use serves to thicken the texture of the speech and give it added authority.

When you find a suitable quotation, be sure to note it correctly.

Great is the scorn of the person who catches a speaker or writer out in a small mistake in a quotation. The Penguin *Book of Quotations* contains around twelve thousand quotes, from Bernard Shaw to the Bible and from Colonel Chinstrap to Franz Kafka. The book is not only useful for checking the exact words, but is also a source of quotations to start you thinking of new facets of the subject of your speech.

Local newspapers can also be an excellent source of speech material. The public library will have file-copies of your local newspapers, and some have clippings, files and indexes which will help you to find the information you want.

If in a bound file you find a key piece of information, on no account cut it out. People do—but men have been hanged for less. Bound files in libraries are sacred, and they are even more sacrosanct in newspaper offices, where the lowest form of abuse is "He's the kind of man who would clip a file!"

Generally you will find the staff of your local newspaper helpful, especially if you time your visit properly.

In the case of a weekly, the best time is often late in the afternoon of the day on which the paper appears. The stress of one week is over, and the work of the following week is not yet looming too large over the horizon. (You may not find all the editorial staff in their offices immediately after press-time, for there are papers where it is not unknown for

LIBRARY

the editorial staff to move *en masse* to the nearest pub as soon as the paper is safely to bed!).

Better, perhaps, to phone and make an appointment if you want detailed information. It is surprising, though, how much a casual browse through the files will yield.

It helps if you know what you are looking for. Newspapermen, whose job is finding information and printing it on the back of advertisements, then selling it, are heart-roasted with requests for free information.

Those requests come from children preparing school projects on a local subject, from people who have been asked to propose the toast to the club at the Angling Club's annual dinner, and from folk who ring up and ask in slurred voices "Shirr, can you tell us who won the Derby in 1949? We've gotta bet on. . . ."

Sometimes when I used to tell a joke my wife would wearily murmur "Reader's Digest 1968!"—but at least I adapted each story to the occasion. If you do not have back-copies of the *Reader's Digest*, keep an eye open for them next time there is a local jumble sale.

"Laughter the best Medicine", "Life's Like That", "Humour in Uniform", and the short fillers at the bottom pages in the Digest can all be used to provide raw material to be worked up into an appropriate story for your own use.

Indeed, the *Reader's Digest* is worth keeping for ready reference. The way I do it is to staple to the appropriate page a small tag with a key-word on it—"Wine", or "San Marino", or whatever it is.

This makes a pile of back-copies look like an untidy paper hedgehog, but it also makes a mass of knowledge readily available at one riffle through the tags.

If you want detailed information on a topic, head for your public library.

Unless you are singularly unlucky you will find the staff friendly and helpful—though usually busy—and willing to guide you in the direction of books and periodicals on the subject of your forthcoming speech.

Through the borrowing service, you have access to over 100,000 books—enough to fill more than thirteen miles of tight-packed shelving.

It is worth while to become familiar with Dewey and his decimal system for cataloguing every field of knowledge.

What is not available in the library in book form or in bound files may be available on micro-film.

Supposing you are speaking on a subject with a key date —maybe the discovery in 1884 of MacTavish's Patent Haggis Harpoon. Look at the *Dictionary of Dates*, and at newspaper files for that year, and you will learn what was happening at the time (and maybe at the very moment) when MacTavish first sent his powered harpoon hurtling towards the unsuspecting haggis.

The Times indexes run back to 1790 and are available in the bigger libraries.

The *Encyclopaedia Britannica*, available in every library, has clues for thousands of speeches in its pages.

Many libraries have a cuttings file on local events and this can be very useful in finding the background to, say, treacle-mining in the Dales.

Every year H. M. Stationery Office publishes thousands of books, pamphlets and leaflets on a great range of subjects, and in building up your own reference library you should consider buying the HMSO publications on your theme.

Again, a great deal of information is to be had for the asking. Find an old treacle-miner, get him on his own at a corner table in the pub, and he will tell you more about the lively background to treacle-mining in an evening than you would learn in a month from textbooks. At every level there are people waiting to be asked for information by sensible inquirers. Museums, trade organisations, Citizens' Advice Bureaux—ask a question and you will almost always get a civil answer.

When assembling the facts for your speech, remember how easy it is to "personalise" it.

A phone-call to the chairman, and a discussion with him about the purpose of the meeting and the kind of people you will be addressing may be enough. If you are making an important speech away from home, a subscription to the local paper for a couple of weeks before the Big Day can be very useful; from those papers you can glean two or three pieces of local knowledge, and the audience are pleased and flattered when they hear you mention with some knowledge the new school or the problem of smoke pollution in the east part of the town—it shows that you have taken them seriously as an audience and done your homework for them.

Any audience takes it as a compliment. Doing your homework even for a vote of thanks is worth while, if you do so without making it too long-winded. For example, you can go to the slight trouble of looking up the speaker's surname in *The Penguin Dictionary of Surnames* and—where the derivation is complimentary—work it into your material.

"Mr. Smith, though the holder of the commonest name in England, has shown us that he is an uncommonly good speaker. A Smith is someone who smites—and Mr. Smith has hammered home his point very skilfully tonight. I am sure none of us will pass a derelict treacle-mine from now on without pondering on what he has told us."

Another way you can show that you have done your homework is to find a little about the personalities on the platform with you. If you can say "Mrs. Hainsworth, who has been president of your organisation for a quarter of a century, will agree with me when I say that to be in charge of an organisation in those early years was none too easy", then you have built a bridge between you and your audience, who know Mrs. Hainsworth and have known her for up to twenty-five years, but do not know you.

But check names and their pronunciation. You may be forgiven for missing out a couple of thousand pounds in a speech, but it will take you longer to live down the fact that you called the chairman "George Chillimondelly-Smith" when his Christian name was William and his surname was pronounced Chumley-Smythe.

Often you can check up on someone by looking up the appropriate reference book, but do not simply pass on the entry from "Who's Who in Treacle-Mining" undigested. Think about the facts and see how they can be applied locally. "Sir John, who was born in 1908" is all right, but "Sir John, who was born in the year that the Longbank Treacle Mine was sunk, 1908", is a great deal better.

It needs work? Yes, but not as much as you would think at first sight. A little imagination goes a long way.

A small "in" joke about a personality in the organisation you are addressing is another bridge-builder, but make sure that the story is accurate and not likely to offend anyone. "I felt, Mr. Chairman, just about as uncomfortable as you did when they fished you out of the sea at the club outing!" If you are going to do this, do it well—nothing sounds more lame and artificial than an attempt at an "in" joke that does not come off.

Again, you can build bridges by taking the trouble to read one or two back copies of the publications devoted to the organisation's purposes or trade. You may not understand what a treacle-miner's double-flanged under-strapped grommet is, but if you incorporate into your speech one or two phrases or stories it will indicate that at least you have gone to the trouble to learn a little about the way the members of the audience spend their working hours.

"The other day, I see, a miner in south Durham came across a nugget of treacle weighing three hundredweights and so pure that it needed no refining. I hope that in my speech you, like that miner, will find one or two worthwhile nuggets. . . ."

If you intend to try to persuade the folk out there in the Woodyard of the rightness of your cause, remember the axiom that "He who asserts must prove." Why should they accept the views you express, just on your say-so?

They may be persuaded by "Let me give you an instance"—followed by examples.

Or as advertisers have proved repeatedly, they will accep- reinforcing opinions in the form of testimonials. The advertising agencies would not shell out big sums to public figures to endorse their clients' products if they were not convinced that testimonials are regarded by the woman in the street as some kind of proof.

Or you can muster figures to back up your assertions. Figures which are gently rounded are more memorable. Not £5,543,189, but "Five and a half million!"

When you quote some authority to back up your assertions, you can add weight to the quotation by saying a little about the expert—you may find the information you want on the cover of one of his books or in the introduction, or you may have to turn to "Who's Who in Treacle-Mining".

Be wary of masses of figures, however gently rounded, either when you are a speaker or when you are a listener.

Use too many statistics in a speech and you may find that your audience has completely lost the thread of what you were trying to put across. This can be done deliberately.

Once I cornered a speaker after a Council meeting and said, "You produced any amount of figures there, but they didn't mean what you said they meant." He laughed without shame. "You know that, I know that, but these stupid ——s in there don't know that!"

Give plenty of thought to the title of your speech, following the example of the writer who spends as much time thinking of the perfect catchy title for a story as he does on the writing; or newspaper sub-editors who devote more time to the headlines than to the story under them.

My own favourite from my files is the title for a speech which I could have simply called "The advantages of blending wines for their mutual improvement."

Instead I called it "You can always marry your mistakes"—and found that from the moment they heard the title the audience were interested, amused, and ready to listen appreciatively.

Try to prepare your speech at least a few days before you need to—though this is often a counsel of perfection. Then lay it to one side for a brief cooling-off period. When you come back to it, and go over the text or outline, you will not only notice mistakes. You will notice omissions, and will be taken aback to find that some important aspects of the speech, which were quite clear in your mind when you wrote the notes, were never translated into words and recorded on the paper at all!

In preparing your speech, remember GIGO. The computer industry has developed a large vocabulary of its own, and one piece of jargon deserves to be taken into the English language. It is the mysterious four-letter word, GIGO.

It means "Garbage in, garbage out". You cannot expect a computer to provide you with good results if you feed it mathematical garbage.

The same applies, in trumps, to speech-making. Good

speeches are based on sound facts and sense; even with the lightest of light-hearted speeches if you only feed garbage in you will get garbage out.

But making up a speech and delivering it is an immensely complicated process, far beyond the capabilities of any computer yet devised. To house the memory that we draw on when we start thinking out our speech would need a computer big enough to fill the Albert Hall. We house all that data in the space between our ears.

Any speech can be made more interesting by remembering the most important subject in the world.

If you and your neighbours were asked to make a list of the subjects that interested you most, and the answers were put in systematic order, the results would be fascinating.

Sex would be high up the list; so would money; so would religion. Sport, wine-making, Indian cookery—they might all be represented. But the list would hardly be valid, for if the average person answered truthfully his answer would be "Myself!"

Your toothache is of more interest to you than an earthquake in Peru, and your own overdraft than the fate of shipbuilding on the Clyde.

Any speech can be made more interesting, then, by remembering the most important subject in the world to your listeners—themselves. Make the speech relate to them, to their hopes and fears, likings and fortunes.

With the Aid of Aida

If you can weave the facts of a speech into a logical sequence, it helps you and the listeners to remember it.

The simplest framework is chronological—the "And what happened next?" method. You start as far back in time as you need to, then take events in order right up to the end of the story.

It is, for example, the most direct way of describing the way a factory works. You start with the raw material dropping off at the loading-bays, and follow its fortunes until, as a finished product, it is packed and shipped.

An obvious idea? You would say so—but how often have you heard a speaker stop and say "No, but before that . . .' or "I might have mentioned that. . . ." Phrases like that are a clue that something in his speech has slipped out of sequence.

Or you can discipline your fact with the help of Rudyard Kipling's Honest Serving-men. In the Just-So Story, "The Elephant's Child", the verse appears—

> I keep six honest serving-men
> (They taught me all I knew)
> Their names are What and Why and When
> And How and Where and Who.

Let's suppose that you are faced with preparing a speech on Treacle-mining in Yorkshire in the Middle Ages—the kind of speech any of us might be called on to make.

Here are just some of the items which could be mustered under each of the six honest serving-men.

What treacle-mining involves in machinery, and in danger.

Why treacle is generally mined, and not worked open-cast.

When treacle-mining first became economically significant.

How treacle was first mined, and how methods improved as the years passed.

Where in Yorkshire treacle was mined, and where you can still see the pit-banks and the ruins of medieval treacle-mines.

And often the most interesting—who! Guy of Bradford, the renegade monk who devised the unspillable treacle-bucket. Grimm Black, the first capitalist treacle-mine owner.

As you can imagine, Kipling's six serving-men can easily be recruited when you are organising the facts for practically any kind of speech, even one that seems on the face of it to be emotional rather than factual.

Any system of organisation is better than producing clumps of unconnected thoughts. A speech should be like a string of beads, with the "beads" linked by a logical thread. The connection can be made by linking-words like "However", "in addition", "On the contrary," "In contrast to this".

A little thought on the natural order of the parts of your speech can make listening much easier for your audience—and makes the speech much simpler to remember.

Remember the good example of Aida. Aida is not a curvaceous blonde, but a friend to salesmen and advertising men.

Aida stands for: Attract attention
Arouse Interest
Create Desire
Ask for Action

To take an example. You are to appeal on the radio for funds for the Yorkshire Society of Destitute Treacle Miners. Briefly, remembering Aida, you might—

Attract Attention—"Remember the luscious treacle puddings you enjoyed as a child. Awd Tom Malham was one of the men who in the days of his strength hewed the treacle which went into those puddings . . . but now . . ."

Arouse Interest—by giving an account of the working life of Awd Tom, and describe the present conditions of his wife and family.

Create Desire—by building up the picture so that the listeners sitting by their radios say, "Eeh, we must do something for those old folks. Down to selling their ration of free treacle from door to door! What a shame!"

Ask for Action—by giving clearly and repeatedly the address to which donations can be sent.

That last step, asking for action, might seem to be the most obvious one of all, the one which would never be overlooked. In fact, many a speaker works his audience up into a fair state of excitement and then leaves them there with no place to go!

If you want people to act, tell them what you suggest they should do.

(This obvious step is overlooked quite often by salesmen. They do everything to arouse interest and create desire, and then fail to place the order-form under the customer's nose and ask for his signature.)

That action part of Aida . . . I like the story of the missionary a thousand years ago who told a gathering of heathens in moving terms about the trial and death of Jesus. Overcome by the vividness of the scene in his mind's eye, the pagan chief seized his war-axe and roared to his men: "Come on, lads, and we'll slaughter the bastards who did that to our Saviour!"

Don't expect, every time you use the help of Aida, to get quite such an emphatic response!

The Handy Idiot Card

I invented the idiot-card for myself, only to find later that other people had been using something similar for years.

The idiot-card, as I use it, is a piece of white cardboard, stiff but not too thick.

On the left-hand side is a column of single words. They mean a great deal to me, though not much to the casual eye.

Let me hunt up the idiot-cards from a recent speech. The words down the left of one card are JELLY BLANKET TIRELESS FIRE BATTLE. Armed with those words I could remember the sequence of ten minutes' speech. On the right-hand side, printed in small capital letters, is an expansion of the single word. This little paragraph still looks cryptic to anyone who is not in the secret.

Certainly I do not attempt to write out the speech in full on the idiot-card though it may well summarise the entire text of a speech previously written out in detail and put away in a drawer.

I use both sides of each idiot-card, numbering the sides in sequence, but some speakers find it less confusing to use one side only.

I have never yet met an audience who showed the slightest objection to notes, held inobtrusively in one hand and referred to as needed. Those firm cards are much more manageable on the platform than sheaves of onion-skin paper that rattles, or technicolor scraps, or sheets as big as single-bed blankets.

When preparing my idiot-cards I take great care to make them clearly legible—it is disconcerting to glance down at the card for the word which will give you the clue for the next couple of minutes of your speech, and find that you are looking at a word which means nothing to you.

"WARVE! What the heck is a warve?" You have missed your stride, however briefly, and have to look to the right at the more detailed notes, to discover that "warve" is really "marble" badly printed.

Idiot-cards are much more compact and manageable than typescripts. The idiot-cards for a series of lectures lasting eighteen hours in total make a pack an inch and five-eighths thick. I have just measured them—and am a little surprised to find that the sheaf was even as thick as that.

An improvised idiot-card can be very useful when you are called on unexpectedly to speak. Even if you have only five minutes to prepare, you can arrange your thoughts in some kind of logical order and by noting down key words you will be reminded not to miss out any essential points.

A small card or the back of an envelope can be used if you have one, but I have found that notes made with a ball-point pen on the back of my left hand are even better. Notes jotted down on a piece of paper can be lost, but so far I have never lost the back of my left hand.

The method works like a kind of conjuring trick. The audience can see that you are speaking without notes, yet changing tacks confidently with one glance at the back of your hand. It helps to build your confidence too—and anything which adds to your confidence when you are on your feet and speaking is well worth doing.

When you are finished, a quick wipe removes the ballpoint notes.

It is better to remember to do this, or you may find yourself asked (as I have been) "What on earth are those words written on the back of your hand for?"

Sometimes the use of idiot-cards is inappropriate—sometimes you cannot avoid reading a speech, because the material in it is important and is being read into the record, so you must be word-perfect.

If you sit down and write a speech like an essay, and then

" . . . *I've never lost the back of my left hand* . . . "

deliver it, it will sound like an essay (which it is) and not like a speech. One way to avoid this stiffness is to prepare notes for your speech, then dictate the full text into a tape-recorder and have it transcribed.

You can then tidy the manuscript a little, and use the transcription as the text of the speech to be carefully read. Your exact words will still go on record, but they will at least sound like a speech as they are read.

On your working copy of the speech, the one which is for your own eye, you can mark in the scoring.

I use a blue ballpoint for this, putting in a thin oblique line between phrases where I want to be reminded to pause briefly, and two thicker lines where I wish to pause longer.

Words or phrases which I want to remember to stress I underline with red ballpoint. And, in the margin opposite each paragraph, and again in red, I print a key word which will remind me of the contents of the paragraph at a glance.

Sometimes (because this copy is very much for my eye alone) I add a reminder about stance and gesture—though never to the extent of the bye-gone orator who noted on his script "At this point, clasp hands chest-high and raise indignant eyes to Heaven."

And, if you are to give a speech from a written text, make sure that it is legible. A clearly typed manuscript is best; failing that, print out in block capitals what you are to say, leaving ample space between the lines and paragraphs.

You may have noticed, watching an important meeting on television, that the main speaker is at the rostrum laying down the law, but the reporters are sitting reading. Why are they not furiously noting his words of wisdom? Because they have the full text of his speech on the desk in front of them, and they are following it carefully to make sure that he does not try to slip one past them by departing from the hand-out on any vital point.

It is a curious fact, and I have noticed it time and again, that many a speech which is thrilling and memorable when delivered, reads flat and dull when you first look through the hand-out.

So, when you have prepared your speech, do not be too disappointed if it does not read as well as you had hoped. It is waiting for you to breathe life into it on the platform.

And remember, too, that you are very familiar with every word in that speech by the time you come to deliver it. It has lost any freshness it ever had for you, but the folk in the Woodyard are hearing it for the first time and will react freshly to it.

When you first begin making speeches, a five-minute speech seems endless. With practice, you find that quarter of an hour is not too difficult. And I have known people who become so much at ease on a platform that they have to be pulled down after an hour and a quarter.

The ideal length of a speech depends on many factors; the old advice of "Stand up, speak up, and shut up" has a lot to commend it. Often the problem can be solved in advance by a word with the Chairman—"How long would you like me to speak?" With any luck you will be given a clear figure—"About a quarter of an hour", or whatever. Sometimes, though, the answer is "Just suit yourself!"

Unless you are the principal speaker (when you may have to talk for an hour or more, depending on the occasion) quarter of an hour is a happy compromise. With luck, that length of speech will tire neither you nor your listeners.

Though running over time is by far the commonest fault with beginners, you can err in the opposite direction. I have been guilty of this only once, but it sticks in my mind.

One of the religions in Scotland is curling; it has not so many followers as the two major religions of football and golf, but its devotees are, if anything, more fanatical. When they speak of brushwork they are not speaking of house-painting or landscape art, they are praising someone's skill with a besom on the ice; and to them a hog is a target area, and not a pig.

Anyway, many years ago I was received into this brotherhood with the appropriate ceremony of passwords and ritual, and was called upon to reply to the toast to the "New-made Curlers". This I did in a speech lasting, I suppose, about a minute.

As I sat down, I realised that there was a noticeable atmosphere of disappointment in the big room. My brother curlers had just sat back to enjoy what they hoped would be about ten minutes of moderately enjoyable humour and there I was—finished.

The speech had been good enough, with a couple of apposite stories in it, but it had been far too short and the audience were disappointed because they felt they had been short-changed.

One of the tasks which not even an experienced speaker tackles with any enthusiasm is to deliver a speech written by someone else, without the chance to read it through several times and make it his own.

The example which comes to mind is a Burgh Treasurer presenting his rating statement. This is passed to him by the town's chief financial officer, and he has to deliver it to the Council as if he had written it himself. This rarely works—he comes to a phrase like "the cost/labour ratio" which he has not met before, and his difficulty makes the device quite obvious.

If you find yourself delivering someone else's speech at short notice, do not attempt to put it over as if it was original. Be content to read it into the record, with enough inflection to make it interesting—read it in fact the way you would read a worthwhile passage out of a book, to a friend.

The case is quite different if someone has written the speech for you and given it to you in time to do your homework. Then, you can rehearse it, and probably alter any phrases that seem awkward and unnatural. You may even go further and prepare idiot-cards so that you can deliver the speech as if it was really your own work.

I am sometimes called on to write speeches for people who have not much confidence, and I try to match the style with what I know of the person who is to deliver it. I have never achieved the high American rates of pay for speech-writing—but neither have I suffered from the speech-writer's nightmare of attending a conference at which I have not only written the principal speeches but also all the replies.

Get it Taped

If I have an important speech to deliver, I type out the whole text of it—trying to remember that it is a speech and not an article—then I score it for pauses and emphasis.

I set up my tape-recorder in a room where I know I will not be interrupted. Then, feeling a bit of a fool, I deliver the speech exactly as I hope to do it on the Great Day.

If I make a mess of it (and I seldom get it right the first time) I wipe the tape and do it again until I have it as I want it.

Then I play the tape back, reading the text carefully at the same time, so that I am learning through eyes and ears.

When I am sure that the speech is very much as I want it, I prepare idiot-cards and hear the recording through once or twice while following the cue-words on the cards.

After that, I play the tape over and over again. I may be lying dozing in my bath, or reading in bed, but the tape goes on and on.

The result is that when I come to speak on the Great Day the words are well imprinted on my memory; it is easier to follow the tram-lines of the prepared text than to switch away from it—and if I do "dry" I have the idiot-cards to prompt me.

This full treatment is reserved only for special speeches nowadays. Often I find that a good deal of thought, and the preparation of the necessary idiot-cards, are all I need when I am to speak on a familiar subject.

When tape-recording a speech, make sure that your text is

typed or written on soft paper. This soft cheap paper does not crackle when turned.

This is useful to remember whenever you have to use a mike. The crackle is disconcerting on a tape-recording made for your own use; it is even more disconcerting if heard during the speech itself, or when you are talking on the radio.

Ordinary blank newsprint, the kind of paper your newspaper is printed on, is very suitable but does not stand up to rough handling and yellows if left around. If you want to keep a speech and use it again and again, revert to stiff white cards; they too will not crackle, since they do not bend when handled.

The more speaking I do, and listen to, the more misgivings I have about learning speeches parrot-fashion, for the more you depend on pure memory the more difficult you make it to think on your feet.

An unexpected question—even just a hacking cough from someone in the front rows of the Woodyard—and you can be thrown out of gear and find it difficult to resume.

I saw a very striking example of this at a recent Burns Supper. The orator, who was proposing the main toast to "The Immortal Memory of Robert Burns", had done his homework very thoroughly. He had written out the complete text of his address, had memorised it and had left it at home.

He started away confidently, then a small interruption from a man the worse of drink at another table threw him off his line of thought. He stumbled, was prompted by his wife, stumbled again and at last had to sit down, to hearty sympathetic applause.

It does not always work out as badly as that. I have heard speeches the best part of an hour long recited parrot-fashion word-perfect. They may not have been lively, but they were memorials to an impressive amount of diligence.

Some people recommend rehearsing speeches in front of a full-length mirror, so that they can ensure that every movement, every gesture, is as they want it.

I pass the idea on to you for your consideration. For

myself, I don't do it. My sense of humour gets in my way.

All right, so Abe Lincoln was also bony, gangling and untidy; modest as I am, I cannot compare myself with Abe while I rehearse a speech. A glimpse of myself when I comb my hair or brush my face is one thing, but to spend hours looking at myself speaking to myself in a mirror. . . .

Talk in Pictures

Commando heroes for ever snarling from behind their guns; heroines for ever looking up into rugged faces; Batman swooping on the cringing villains—a look at a newsagent's counter is enough to show that to many people pictures speak louder than words. And this is confirmed by one word —television.

You can use visual aids so that the audience will see what you are trying to put across to them, but you can also paint vivid pictures on the television screens of their minds.

If you express the output of the gasworks in British Thermal Units it means nothing to most of us. But say "The production of gas from our local gasworks is enough to bring the water in the reservoir to the boil in three days" and we have a much clearer mental picture of what all those BTUs can do.

I am an enthusiast for this way of putting ideas across. What is the most far-fetched example I have devised? The "cups of tea" story, perhaps.

My speech was about the importance of the railway to local sugar-beet producers. I phoned the station and found out in round figures how many tons of beet were loaded at the station annually. I knew the approximate percentage of sugar one obtains from raw beet, so I phoned a friend in a big canteen and asked her how much sugar they allowed for every hundred cups of tea. She did not know offhand, but checked the figure and phoned me back.

All this, so that in my speech I could hammer home the importance of rail freight by saying "From that one station goes enough sugar beet to sweeten two cups of tea for every man, woman and child in Britain."

The effectiveness of talking in pictures is shown by the way a woman spoke to me in the street. She stopped me and said "You're the wallpaper man, aren't you?"

I had a bizarre mental picture of myself in white overalls hanging wallpaper—bizarre, because it is a job I just cannot do successfully—and I must have looked slack-jawed and taken aback, for she twinkled and said "I'm sorry but I always do think of you as the Wallpaper Man. You remember you spoke to the Woman's Guild about the early books of the Bible?"

I did remember. Thanks to an agnostic teacher who, honest man, could not give religious instruction during the Religious Instruction period at school, but spoke instead on the early manuscripts of the Bible, I developed an interest in the way we got that amazing library of history, poetry, myth and moral advice. I can speak with reasonable accuracy on the subject, and I sometimes do. And when I speak about the scrolls which were used before books were devised, I say "Just imagine how difficult it would be to read a book printed on a roll of wallpaper."

The lady in the street had almost certainly forgotten whatever I had said about the Codex Siniaiaticus, but she had remembered the mental picture of the roll of wallpaper.

A useful way to think up a good "picture" illustration is to use the words "If they were laid end to end, they would stretch from here to. . . ."

Supposing we are speaking on the subject of wine (a very frequent subject of mine in public speeches and private conversation) and we want to get across the sheer vastness of the gallonage of wine produced and drunk every year.

Taking the world production of wine as 2,600 million gallons a year, what can we do with the figure? Just to stand up and say "You may be surprised to hear that every year two thousand six hundred million gallons of wine are made throughout the world, give or take a glass or two" is not going to convey much.

My attitude to figures like that is, I suspect, pretty common. I am like the Bushman who counts "One. Two. Three. A lot.

A Hell of a lot!" and that figure of wine production simply means "A Hell of a lot!"

If we use the end to end technique, what can we come up with? There are six bottles of wine in a gallon, so we end up with an even bigger figure—15,600,000,000 if my basic arithmetic is right.

A gallon, though, is merely a unit of measurement; a bottle is a thing, and we can put bottles end to end.

Happily for the simplicity of the arithmetic, a wine-bottle is almost exactly a foot long—I have just taken a ruler to the wine-cellar and checked. Divide, and keep on dividing, and we find that our original figure of the annual world production of wine, if translated into bottles laid end to end, would stretch for 2,954,545 miles. Another large and nobbly figure, so we cheat a bit and round it up to three million.

Now let your imagination take over.

"Imagine the world production of wine in bottles. The bottles, laid end to end, would stretch from here to the moon twelve times."

"So much wine is made in the world annually that if it was bottled and laid end to end, the line would go round the equator a hundred and twenty times!"

"Most of the world's wine comes from small vineyards. Imagine a father handing over his vineyard to his son after thirty years, a generation in fact. In that time, enough wine will have been made in the world to stretch bottled from the vineyard to the sun!"

The final impression that the audience is left with is still the Bushman's "A Hell of a lot!"

But we can bring that figure nearer home.

Let's go back and have a look at the gallonage.

When I have a bath, I sometimes take the opportunity to fill winemaking vessels full of scalding water from the tap and let it cool to a comfortable temperature then pour it into the bath. That way, I clean the vessels *and* myself. And I know that twenty-five gallons gives a nice deep bath.

That's better.

"The world production of wine is two thousand six hundred million gallons a year. That doesn't sound much if you say it quick, but it is enough to give you and me and every other person in Britain two good deep baths in wine!"

Those illustrations should not pepper every speech, but one or two of them worked into a speech at least show that you have done your homework—which the people in the Woodyard always take as a compliment.

Sometimes you can use the same format less seriously—"If all the drunks in this county were laid end to end nobody would be a bit surprised."

The best-known example of "talking in pictures" are the parables of Jesus, who took the simple aspects of life in a small town in an agricultural district in which few were very rich or very poor, and made his point time and again by telling us what the farmer and his wife, or the pearl-merchant, or the businessman did.

"We are asked simply to observe that life is like that," says one Biblical scholar. "When we have looked at life as it is, then the meaning of the parable suggests itself to the mind."

We may not wish to begin our word-pictures with "Once upon a time a man went off into a far country", but we can use parables with great effect just the same.

You can draw your "parables" from your own family. The average person out there in the Woodyard is much more interested in what your Uncle Willie did when the rat ran up his trouser-leg than he is in some abstract quotation from Karl Barth—and with a little contriving you can teach the same lesson through the lively word-picture.

Real or fictitious—I admit to creating a whole busload of imaginary relatives to suit my purpose.

Once again, you are not on oath. It's a pity if excessive reverence for the facts prevents you from teaching the truth. . . .

When you are sitting on a bus and you realise that you can hear the conversation of the couple behind you, what do you do?

You deliberately do your best to shut out what is being said?

I don't believe you!

People are endlessly curious about other folk's conversation, and they enjoy almost as much a rehearsal of what someone else has been saying. You know the kind of remark ". . . and he said that she had told him that, and then he said. . . ."

You can make use of this in illustrating a talk. Instead of simply making a blunt statement—"Treacle-mining is becoming increasingly dangerous!"—you can turn it into reported dialogue—

"I met the Safety Officer of United Treacle Mines the other day, and I remarked that his job must be growing easier and easier.

"Not at all," he told me sharply.

"I'd have thought that modern methods were bound to be safer?" I suggested.

But he tells me that modern shearing machinery increases the chance of serious injury. In the old days, a careless worker ran the risk of being hit on the ankle by his own shovel, but now if he tangles with a treacle-shearer he is a hospital case for sure. "The trouble is that even experienced treacle-miners tend to underestimate the time it takes to wade out of the way of a down-coming shearer," he explained.

Everyone dreams. Some people are unaware of the dreams when they wake, but all of us spend up to a third of our lives in "dream-time".

Our own dreams are fascinating. They are, after all, one of the peep-holes into our own subconscious worlds. Other people's dreams? Less interesting if told at length.

Yet a well-selected dream can make a memorable and vivid illustration in a speech.

The hall is warm, the audience are themselves nodding on the edge of "dream-time" and suddenly you say "I never thought I would walk down the High Street with not a stitch of clothes on, and not feel embarrassed." Or "I always thought pink elephants were a rather grubby pink, and not that lovely luminous pink"—and the audience is back with you.

Of course the dream must be built into the speech and not just told for its own sake.

Open confession is good for the soul. My own dream life is vivid and generally very enjoyable, but I have been known to invent a dream to suit the speech I was preparing. Who's to know? After all, our dreams are completely private!

Once more, you are not on oath and are not really cheating unforgivably if you make up a dream for a purpose. My favourite, which I have been able to quote more than once, was a fictitious dream about trying to suck a dead mouse up with a vacuum cleaner.

You can draw on your own imagination for illustrations. Some years ago, speaking of the need for blood donors, I painted as lurid a picture as I could of an imaginary accident. A young motor cyclist had run out of road on a bad bend; he had escaped unscathed, but his sweetheart on the pillion was badly hurt.

Even so, she might have been saved if blood of her group had been available.

And there was the young motor cyclist looking at the audience and asking "Did she die just because you would not be bothered to give blood?"

Some time after, when I went to give a donation of blood, a woman came up to me and told me angrily, "I didn't mean to come. I didn't want to come. But I kept thinking about that young motor cyclist."

The vivid picture had done what I am sure no amount of exhortation could have achieved.

On the same subject—an accident in a distillery some years ago gave a great "picture". A young man was trapped in a screw mechanism so thoroughly that they had to cut the machinery to pieces to get him out. Skilled surgery saved the use of his leg—but he would not have lived to walk again if he had not received massive blood transfusions while he was trapped.

And that young man, as soon as he was fit, queued to give blood so that he could in part repay his debt.

The imaginary young man sorrowing for his sweetheart, and the real young man grateful for his life, are the kind of material from which you can construct the word-pictures which effectively get your message across.

The way in which extra details can be employed to give added impact is shown by Winston Churchill's graphic account of being knocked down by a car in New York. He does not say that the car struck him forcefully—he says "It was the equivalent of falling thirty feet on to a pavement . . . I do not understand why I was not broken like an eggshell or squashed like a gooseberry."

Conscious exaggeration is another useful device, especially in debate. "My opponent is exaggerating again. I must have told him a million times not to exaggerate."

You can leaven your entire speech by bringing in unexpected and vivid similes. Avoid cliches—we all know by this time that pancakes are flat, that judges are sober and lords are drunk. It takes a little more work to come up with something original. (Towards More Picturesque Speech in the *Reader's Digest* may give you some ideas, though some of the examples are rather far-fetched.)

An example of this vivid speech cropped up on the radio as I wrote this—"You can see that on the haunted fishtank tonight," says Tony Blackburn—a simile which makes you think slightly differently about television.

Sometimes a little audience participation can illustrate a point more memorably than any amount of exhortation. You are speaking about different forms of energy. "Everybody clap. No, louder than that! Your palms are stinging and perhaps you are still aware of your arm muscles—but the energy you all put into that applause was not enough to produce even a feeble glow in an electric light bulb."

Or an illustration I have used myself. "Take a deep breath. I have been speaking about the presence of yeast cells in the air. Well, you have just breathed in enough yeast cells to start a brewery". The snag about that picture is that afterwards I have seen members of the audience sitting puce in the face, trying not to inhale more yeast cells.

Be specific in your pictures. "He was a friendly man. In fact, effusive and over-friendly at times," conveys a picture. "He was so friendly that he jumped up on everyone like a six-month-old Labrador puppy" shows us the man even more vividly.

A Pig in Bed

The barrack-room was chilly and bleak. "I'm cauld. I wish I had a pig in bed with me!" said one of my fellow Scots.

"You Jocks don't take a pig to bed with you on cold nights?" one of the English soldiers exclaimed.

"Aye, sometimes two. Do you no' have pigs in England?"

"Yes, but we don't even allow them in the house, never mind putting one in the bed!"

This went on for a while, and I lay biting my tongue and trying not to laugh out loud. To the Scots lad, a pig (in that context) was an earthenware hot water bottle. To the English lad . . . well, you can see why he had no notion to take a pig to bed with him, no matter how chilly the barrack-room was.

The pig which caused the confusion is a good example of the pitfall of using dialect or trade jargon to an audience who does not understand it. When in doubt, use the equivalent word in standard English.

But if you cut out dialect altogether you lose some of the vitality you can bring to a speech.

A Yorkshire treacle-miner addressing a gathering of his fellow workers would be entitled to use a broad Yorkshire tongue and to bring in, without explanation, the jargon of the treacle-mine pit face. If a stranger was present, he might feel he was drowning in verbal treacle as he listened to references to "t'owd treeeacle-gradin' snoober".

The same treacle-miner, addressing a Yorkshire audience with few treacle-miners in it, might still be very obviously Yorkshire in his speech, but would use fewer trade terms and would explain briefly the terms he did use.

Send the treacle-miner south to London to represent his Union on a parliamentary committee, and he would use standard English and make sure that every word relating to the treacle-miner's craft was clearly explained.

It would, I feel, be a pity if he abandoned even in the Palace of Westminster all traces of his Yorkshire accent. A man who irons away every hint of his native accent seems ashamed of the rock from which he was hewed.

But the danger of puzzling or misleading an audience because of dialect or specialised jargon must be kept in mind.

The danger of using dialect words which are not familiar to most of your listeners is related to that of indulging in the use of too many long and unfamiliar words.

Whatever kind of accent or dialect you use, or whatever level of literary English you adopt, the first and most important quality of a speech is clarity—people should know, without racking their brains, what you mean.

The second essential quality is clarity.

The third essential quality is clarity.

And after you have achieved those three essential qualities you can take your pick of the rest, and put them in what order you please.

"I just seemed to run out of words," said a friend shamefacedly when he came back to the seat beside me. He had been scheduled to speak for twenty minutes, but spoken for only ten.

"Run out of words!" That sad phrase stuck in my mind. Surely you cannot possibly run out of words?

Talking at an average speed of a hundred words a minute, a man of poor vocabulary could run through his entire word-list in twenty minutes, for he may manage happily on only two thousand words.

Shakespeare would have taken just over a day—his vocabulary has been estimated at fifteen thousand words.

But even fifteen thousand words is only a fraction of the total available. Start reading out the words defined in a large dictionary, and it will be a month reading day and night before you stumble past zircon, zombie, zoril and Zulu to the end.

So there is no need to run out of words.

I shudder, however, at the advice sometimes given to writers and speakers. They are, according to this advice, to memorise large slabs of the dictionary, of Roget's Thesaurus, and the *Dictionary of Synonyms and Antonyms*. But no one ever developed a simple, lucid and easy style in this artificial way.

One of the great aids to building up a real working vocabulary is to read the kind of books and articles which you personally enjoy, which mean something to you—and not to let unfamiliar words in those books and articles slip by unquestioned and undefined.

One local politician who had perfected his English in the "swallow the dictionary" way was very hurt when I told him one day that this method was the very opposite to mine. "You go through a sentence picking out all the small words and sticking big ones in. I go through a sentence picking the big words out and sticking small ones in!"

If a long word is *right*, and if you feel as happy using it as a good craftsman feels when using a familiar tool, then by all means use it.

But remember that a reader can take a second squint at an unfamiliar long word on the printed page and can tease a meaning out of it by re-reading the context. The spoken word comes not again; the listener has no leisurely chance to solve any puzzles.

Part of the difficulty of being natural on a platform is that you tend to feel that you must speak in more high-flown English than you would use in conversation.

This comes naturally to some people, but not to others. I could not use (with a straight face) the sentence "I regret to intimate the absence of Councillor Blank through temporary indisposition" and would be tempted to rephrase it "I'm sorry that Councillor Blank cannot be here tonight—he is off ill."

There used to be a rule which English teachers stressed; they called it "elegant variation" and they drummed into their pupils that they must not use the same word twice in a paragraph.

Their pupils went out into the wide world, and some of them produced the kind of newspaper English in which the ball in a football match becomes the sphere the next time it is mentioned and the leather the time after.

Speakers can safely forget the rule—just as sports writers have done.

A key word or phrase deliberately repeated again and again can ram home a point in a way that no amount of elegant variation could achieve.

A hypothetical example—a speech devoted to careless methods of treacle-mining could be punctuated by the repeated paragraph "This goes on every day, yet every day thousands of tons of valuable treacle are lost through slip-shod mining methods."

Too much regard for pedantic grammar can give an impression of stiffness in a speech especially when this excessive correctness is accompanied (as it often is) by longwindedness.

Try not to build up a deserved reputation for being able to say very little in the greatest possible number of words.

Beware, too, of over-long sentences. Here you can learn from my bad example. I tend to trap myself in long involved sentences, spiked with parentheses and interjections which meander along until, like a flash-flood in the Sahara, they just dry up without reaching a destination. Shorter sentences are easier to use and you can draw breath oftener—but do not fall into the opposite error and produce a parody of the *Daily Mirror* machine-gun style.

Nervousness, or a sense of occasion, can make people adopt a very artificial voice—what is called in Scotland "panloaf" or "getting to your English". When you find yourself talking like this, give yourself a figurative shake—why hide behind an artificial voice? You would not consider going on to the platform and speaking behind a false face.

The tape recorder is a great check on this habit.

Make your pronunciation of words as correct as you can, but do not worry too much about mispronouncing one or two. A friend of mine, an honours M.A. and a master of English, always thought that when two vehicles bumped into each other they "collidded".

I knew perfectly well what he meant, and never had the bad manners (or the nerve) to correct him.

Once you realise that the people out there in the Woodyard are your friends you lose the temptation to gabble on; take it easy, you have more time than you think.

Once, for a bet, I worked a pause lasting a minute into the middle of a speech, and got off with it. *You* may be uncomfortably aware of the silence while you wait for a split second for the right word to come to your mind, but no-one else is.

Some people are shy of using the "big I" in speeches, which is a pity. After all, the audience are there to listen to you. That is not an open invitation to unbridled egotism.

In general, unless you are the Queen, the Pope, or an Editor, do not use "we" where you really mean "I". Sometimes of course "We" is right—if for example you are the spokesman of a committee or other body, and have to say "We, the members of the Treacle-miners Amalgamated Union, would remind you that the conditions of service very clearly state that. . . ."

In the same way (as you can see throughout this book) I prefer to use the direct word "you" instead of the less personal and more pedantic "one".

Your friend the tape recorder will check peculiarities of dialect, vocabulary, accent and pace.

The first time you hear yourself, you squirm and think "That can't possibly be me!" The voice is familiar yet strange, because you are hearing it without the muffling effect of your head bones, sinus passages and the like.

Without a tape recorder you can get an impression of your own voice by doing what some folk-singers habitually do—cup a hand behind your ear while speaking. But not on a platform during a speech. . . .

A tape recording of one of your speeches is more valuable than all your acquaintances' good advice in drawing attention to any flaws in delivery. I had been told that I punctuated my speeches with "aaahs" and "and-ehs", but it needed a recording to convince me.

You may find that you too have peculiarities of speech, even if not as extreme as one minister I knew.

He had a fine selection of defects, of which the most obvious was a tendency to hold on to the last word of a sentence.

"Think on those things," he would say, and the "innnnngs" would go ricochetting round the timbers of the kirk roof. He was a saintly man, and his flock put up with his speech defects gladly—but you can be a saint and speak well too; and the candid advice of a tape recorder will help you to spot the flaws.

Helpful Hardware

People learn through their eyes as well as through their ears and, given a suitable subject, speakers can take advantage of this by using visual aids.

Those can take many forms—diagrams on a blackboard, a big wheel graph or pie graph to show how money is allocated; a flannelgraph of the kind used in Sunday Schools to build up pictures a unit at a time; slides, and films.

Those pictures help you to compete with the images on the built-in mental television set in the minds of each member of the audience. The more interesting you can make the illustrations and the word-pictures the more chance there is that you will capture their attention from their own picture-show.

Flip-over cards, with large, clear pictures and lettering, are useful visual aids. Be sure to make them big enough, proportionately to the size of the hall you are speaking in. Nothing elaborate is needed in the way of hinges—good strong string is adequate. But do make sure that you have something solid to hang the wad of cards on, and that they are high enough for everyone to see them clearly.

Very striking visual aids can even detract from your words. In a recent book of mine, the cartoonist cunningly brought a small mouse into every illustration. You know, I am jealous of that mouse! Far too many people speak about him and neglect to mention the brilliant text-matter I wrote between the cartoons!

A vivid way to illustrate a talk is to bring along some of the tools of the trade—a haggis-hunter's harpoon or a treacle-miner's broadbladed pick. But do not pass any small exhibits round the hall while you are talking—the audience are there to listen to you and not to play hunt-the-thimble along the rows.

Besides, you may never see your exhibit again. . . .

When you bring visual aids with you, beware of leaving them on the platform in clear view of the audience, otherwise you will find yourself competing with your own props. When they should be listening to you, the members of the audience are sitting there wondering "How on earth is he going to work a stag's head and a pram handle into a speech on treacle-mining?"

When using visual aids of any kind, remember MacPherson's Law. I do not know who the original MacPherson was, and I suspect that his accident-prone body has been laid to rest long ago in a grave which proved to be two inches too short for the coffin.

It was MacPherson who postulated the Law of Intractability of Inanimate Objects.

To the public speaker this means that any slide which can stick will stick, any object which can melt will melt (that lump of crude treacle-ore will weld itself to the desk-top before you can lift it to display it) and anything which can roll will roll—and will inevitably roll into a dark corner or off the platform down into the audience.

A clever three-dimensional model which has to be unfolded and propped up is the kind to avoid; it will not unfold as it did when you tried it at home, and it will stay propped up until you reach the most important part of your speech and then collapse.

I have had, before now, an impromptu wrestling-match with a six-foot length of rubber tube in front of a large audience—and what could be a simpler prop than that.

So beware of MacPherson's Law. Try to make your visual aids as simple as possible.

Simple visual aids are not only less accident-prone, they are likely to have more impact because of their directness.

Slice your Roast Thin

There is a saying among journalists, "Slice your roast thin." Why cram all your facts into one indigestible article, when you can spread them more profitably over several lighter and more digestible articles?

The same applies to speeches.

When I started speaking on wines and wine-making I used to cover the whole subject in an hour, leaving my audience stupified by the sheer weight of facts and opinions. Now I try to make a more interesting speech on one aspect of that large subject.

If your subject is gardening, do not attempt to give a speech entitled "Gardening". One minor aspect of the subject—growing good tulips, building a rockery, using compost—will be more than enough for one speech.

There are several practical reasons for slicing your roast thin. It makes it more digestible, enabling the listeners to assimilate a number of facts thoroughly, instead of failing to take in an avalanche of information. But, from your point of view, the overwhelming practical reason for slicing it thin is that you will probably be asked back to speak, and it is embarrassing to have to say "I'm sorry. I told you all I know about the subject in that speech."

You may have been making speeches for quite a time before the hard fact hits you that you are now a public speaker in some demand and that this is showing every sign of continuing.

When this horrid revelation, with its prospect of endless meetings and broken evenings, is still fresh in your mind is the time to start arranging your material systematically.

All your speeches, whether complete manuscripts or notes on a number of cards, should go in a file with a note of the contents on the cover. Only in this way, as I know from bitter experience, can you lay hands at short notice on your stock speeches on "Robert Burns and the Deep-mining System of Treacle Production" and "Winemakers can Marry Their Mistakes".

The next step in being systematic is to start a cuttings file. No need for anything elaborate there. I have thousands of cuttings and can find one within a minute or two, yet to a jaundiced eye they look like a heap of waste paper. The clippings are slipped into folders made from a double page out of a gardening magazine, with one key word written on the top margin.

The next step—a card index. When you come across a quotation or a joke which you feel you may be able to use, write it down clearly on a card and put a key-word up at the top. And, in the case of quotations, give the exact and complete source. There is nothing more annoying than having a quotation to your hand, one on which you can build a fine speech, and realise that one key word is not clear and that you cannot go back to the source again and check.

To start with, the meagre files and thin sheaf of cards will seem to mock you, but as the years go by you will find they have grown to a very useful size.

You may even have so much material on your speciality that you end up writing an authoritative book on it.

In any case, amassing more facts than you need for any one speech is not time wasted.

Most journalists have noticed a rather puzzling fact. When you don't know much about a subject, and every fact you know has been pressed into service for the article you are writing, the finished article "reads thin". Yet, when you know a great deal about a subject, and have to leave masses of good material out, the article seems solid and convincing.

How can the presence of facts in reserve show in an article? I cannot figure it out, but it is true. It is true of speeches too.

Blast Off

A striking introduction can be the making of a speech, but only if you have even better material to follow. Count Basie, speaking of playing jazz, once told Tony Bennett, "If you start at the top there's nowhere to go," and the same advice applies to speeches. Do not, in an effort to impress your listeners instantly, cram all your jewels into the first two minutes.

If your speech is intended to be light-hearted and amusing rather than informative, you can hardly say so in your introductory remarks—"This is going to be one long laugh from start to finish!" A neat way of getting the message over is by saying something like "This speech is modelled on a long-horn bull; the points are there all right, but there is a whole lot of bull between the points!"

The calendar can help to give you a striking introduction. You know weeks ahead the date on which you are going to speak. There are several books which will tell you which anniversary falls on the same date and you can adapt the information appropriately.

This can range from the sublime to the ridiculous. Take at random one date—November 6th.

"Mr. Chairman, ladies and gentlemen, before I begin I would like to mention that this is the birthday of the Roman Emperor Julian. Happy birthday Julian, wherever you are!" A ridiculous introduction? Yes, but one which would tell your audience right at the beginning that they would wait in vain if they were expecting a serious speech.

On the same date, November 6th, died Sir James Falstaff, English knight. What a foundation on which to build, on that date, a diatribe against the Common Market, or a dissertation on the Essential English Character, or even an account of the way in which fictional characters come by their names.

Using the date of a speech to provide an appropriate introduction has the great merit that the audience know that this at least is not some old tired piece of work which you are trotting out for the hundredth time.

How can they know that you have tacked this new and appropriate head to the body of an old speech?

Chambers *Book of Days* can be consulted in most public libraries, or sometimes picked up second-hand. As well as listing saints' days and famous births and deaths it is a mine of unusual information which can be worked for speeches on everything from practical jokes to the last words of remarkable persons.

One of the "shock" introductions I use is "In the three hours and twenty minutes which I understand are at my disposal, I can only touch on the main points . . ." The listeners who, up to that point, have prepared themselves for a half-hour speech, sit up with a jerk. They are listening . . . and the fact that you do not actually speak for the full three hours and twenty minutes is a bonus.

Sometimes a commonplace introduction given a new twist has great impact.

Like most ex-Servicemen, I can look back on a succession of speeches by new Commanding Officers, all containing the magic sentence "You play ball with me and I'll play ball with you."

Of them all, only one sticks in my mind. We were drawn up in hollow square on the gravel of the Egyptian desert to hear the words of our new C.O. "You play ball with me and I'll play ball with you," he said, and everyone groaned inwardly. Then he gave a grim smile and added " . . . and I'll still kick you all over the Western Desert!"

At which point everyone started paying attention. And that is the purpose of an introduction.

Splash-down

A public speaker's experience is built up piece by piece over the years, but I can clearly remember the occasion when I realised the importance of knowing when to stop.

The man who was proposing the votes of thanks at a public banquet was a friend of mine and a worthy local politician, but he was a little hazed by whisky and had no clear idea how to pull his speech to a close.

So he went on and on and on. He was simply rambling, but he did not know what to say to release himself from his nightmare.

The guests began to scuffle their chairs. Then they began to scrape their feet, and to chat to each other. At last they gave him the slow hand-clap. And this was at a formal banquet. Yet he still went on and on, until after ninety-five minutes he stumbled to a stop and slumped down.

In that ninety-five minutes I firmly resolved that I would never stand up to speak without knowing exactly how I was going to stop.

Let me advise you: "Even if you have not prepared the rest of the speech in detail, put some work in on your ending."

Usually, having made a mental note of the time I intend to speak, I lay my watch inobtrusively in front of me, and this warns me when I am beginning to go over the limit.

Or you can plant a friend somewhere in the audience to signal when you are running on too long. A noiseless blast on a clean handkerchief can serve as a warning. The same friend, primed in advance, can signal to you if you are

proving inaudible or guilty of any other serious shortcoming.

"This is the way the world ends. Not with a bang but a whimper." The quotation from T. S. Eliot's *The Hollow Men* seems to have been adopted as a motto by some public speakers. Their speeches don't end, they wind slowly down. And then the speaker murmurs "Thank you" (thanking the audience for I know not what), and then they sit down.

You can do much better than that.

You can hardly do worse.

One of the best ways to end a speech is to wind up by telling the audience what you have just told them.

Introduce the summing up with an appropriate phrase—the most obvious and direct is the best, "To sum up. . . ."

"To sum up—unless something is done about the detergent content of soil-water, then treacle-mining in Yorkshire will die out and become merely part of England's industrial history.

"What can you do personally? You can use soap instead of detergent. You can take care not to empty your shaving-water into streams and rivers.

"And what can we do collectively? We can write to our Members of Parliament and persuade them to make the use of detergents a capital offence throughout the length and breadth of treacle-mining Yorkshire."

When you come to recap what you have said, make sure to remind the audience of anything you want them to note down—the name of a book, the date of a meeting, the address of an official. Pause long enough to allow anyone who wishes to look out a piece of paper and note down the information—indeed, encourage them to do this.

No doubt your listeners intend to act on what you have said, but human memory can be fragile and partial. What is noted down is more likely to be taken seriously and acted on.

Someone once said that the best ending to a speech was like the pictures which pass before the eyes of a drowning man—vivid . . .and brief.

And remember the tribe in Nyasaland who silenced any long-winded speakers at village gatherings with shouts of "Imetosha"—"That's plenty!"

At the end of almost every speech comes a vote of thanks. I find this a difficult moment when I am the subject of the thanks.

Well, what do you do? Sit and nod in agreement as you are praised? Gaze mutely at the ground between your feet? Try to avoid a pleased smirk sliding on to your face?

I try to listen to the proposer attentively, and yet look modest.

Most times, I fail.

And votes of thanks can be difficult to propose. Supposing the speech has been far too long and resoundingly dull, common humanity and good manners forbid that you should say so. There is always something kind but true that you can say.

You can, for instance, praise the long-winded man for the obvious care he has taken in preparing a subject near to his heart.

You can thank a dull speaker for his sincerity and his painstaking approach to treacle-mining in Yorkshire . . . it all adds up to an exercise in tact as shown by the politician, who, when given an anonymous and drooling brat to kiss, used to murmur enthusiastically "Now there's a baby!" No argument about that!

And if you are lucky you may find when you come to propose the vote of thanks that in your sheer delight at the high quality of the speech the words will come rushing eloquently from your lips . . . it does sometimes happen like that.

When you have proposed the vote of thanks, make it quite clear that you expect a reaction from the audience—lead the applause.

After you have given a speech which is important to you, and which you feel has put worthwhile information in front of your audience, are you going to stop there, or are you going to try to get that message to a wider audience through the press?

If you see reporters hard at work at a table in the front of the hall all should be well—though it does no harm to have a rèsumè of the speech ready, with the outstanding facts and figures set out in it, to hand to them.

Reporters (being human) are glad of any help they are given, and it is a great assistance in untangling page after page of notes if you have before you the speaker's own idea of what is most worth while in his speech.

The average reporter has a very wide range of general knowedge but cannot be expected to be an expert on every subject. You are speaking, say on treacle-mining, and he is hardly aware that treacle is mined, so how can you expect him to get the point of your description of the new multiple-scoop techniques of open-cast treacle-mining?

Your hand-out will help to ensure that what appears in the press is accurate.

And if the press is not there, then see that the local papers still get the résumé—and as soon as possible. Early copy is almost certain to go in, but, as press-time approaches, the chance gets more and more slim.

Nor should you forget the trade press. Send the rèsumè to the Treacle-Miner's World and Syrup-Quarrier's Gazette.

Generally, a brief résumé of the speech and the circumstances in which it was given is most likely to be published, but when the speech is really important then have the full text duplicated and sent to the press. Then they can take from it what they want—which may be quite different from what you think is significant!—and may quote large chunks of it.

Some people feel that to obtain publicity like this is immodest and undignified. Maybe this is so when it is done for personal glory—though that is a very human desire—but it seems to me entirely laudible when you do so in order to spread your message as widely as possible.

Facing the Box

Sooner or later, if you make a name as a speaker or as an expert in some subject or hobby you are going to be asked to appear on radio or television.

Then perhaps the nervousness you thought was gone for ever will come back with a rush.

I remember vividly the first time I heard myself on the radio. I was a member of a quiz team, and by good luck every question might have been designed for me, I gave answer after answer in a clear confident voice, until I was asked a question that almost every other adult male in Britain could have answered off the cuff.

"Where does the boat race begin and end?"

"Putney to Mortlake."

I know that now, and will never forget it. The names are burned deep in my memory.

The programme was recorded in familiar surroundings and apart from the mikes and technicians could have been an ordinary club night.

But I will always remember the subsequent shock of hearing my own voice on the air. I felt like crawling under the couch. Where on earth did I get that gruff accent that sounded as if it had originated somewhere in the Irish Sea between the west of Scotland and the north of Ireland?

Now that tape recorders are so much commoner, you are likely to get over the shock of hearing yourself speak at a very much earlier stage.

Some years after that quiz, I was called to Broadcasting House to speak about a project I had been involved in. The young lady who was to interview me was very considerate.

She brought me a cup of tea and reassured me about the procedure. I realised that I was being gently soothed.

"Look!" I said, "You'll get plenty of people in here with more mellifluous voices and plenty with more interesting subjects, but you won't get anyone less bothered with nerves!"

"Thank God for that!" she said cheerfully, and pointed to the mike. "Three minutes—and I'll prompt you with a question if you dry up!"

On radio, the audience is conscious only of your subject and your voice. The fact that you are sitting in the studio running your finger round your collar is neither here nor there.

Television, on the other hand, is essentially visual by its nature.

If you are ever asked to appear as the main speaker in a television programme, you will be well coached in what to do and what not to do. But what if you are picked on to appear briefly on the box, as happens day and daily to scores of people?

Remember your eye contact. When you look that goggling lens straight in the eye, you are looking directly at your audience. When you look away, you run the risk of seeming inattentive or even shifty. But don't stare unblinking at that glass eye.

And do stand still! A speaker dodging about so much that the camera man is sea-sick trying to keep him in frame does not impress the viewer.

And if you are seated, sit upright (but not stiffly). You would not go into a stranger's home and flop down in the big armchair and slouch there as you spoke; when you face the camera you are going into the homes of a million strangers.

Once again—sit at peace, and do not offer the viewer a bewildering succession of shots of your left ear, the top of your head and the underside of your chin.

When you appear on the box you and your friends will notice mannerisms you never knew you had.

My favourite mannerism used to be a constant combing action, running the fingers of my right hand through my ample hair. Now, with less hair on top and more on my face, I am conscious sometimes of the habit of pulling my moustache—which is the kind of habit that shows up under the beady eye of the goggle-box.

Potential speakers on radio or television are often advised "Be sincere, because insincerity shows up at a microphone far more than from a platform." That advice is all very well, but if the speaker is a phoney as a fifty-pence note and he is trying to put forward an undeserving cause, what else can he sound but insincere?

Sincerity is not something that you can apply with a make-up brush. It comes from inside.

You can however avoid looking shifty and insincere by remembering to look at the camera, and hence at your audience. You can avoid looking like an inefficient propagandist giving a rehearsed speech in a dead-pan voice. You can avoid the impression of trying to dazzle your listeners with science, by using direct and lucid language, not gobbledegook and jargon.

And the best of luck on the box!

The height of modern fame is to appear regularly on colour television at peak viewing times. That makes you a Television Personality (even if you have nothing much to say) and who could wish a public speaker a better fate than that . . . ?

Forty Shades of Blue

Many books on public speaking tell you flatly "Never tell a story that could offend the most prudish of your audience."

I will not go as far as that, but I must strongly advise any speaker to temper his material so that it is not too blue.

This takes some judgement.

No speaker offended an audience by using material a shade less blue than they expected, but it is sad to see someone ploughing solidly and cold-bloodedly through dirty joke after dirty joke, because he thinks it is expected of him, while the atmosphere in the room grows steadily chillier and chillier and the applause more and more perfunctory.

If only people like that would realise that a blue joke is a joke first and blue only incidentally.

So, though I am not prepared to say "Never tell a blue joke, of however light a shade of blue!" I am prepared to say emphatically, "Never, in any company, tell a joke for dirt's sake!"

You have one yardstick for your choice of jokes. It is this—if you have any misgivings about telling a joke, don't tell it. You will be uncomfortable as you tell it, and will infect your audience with your uneasiness.

The same joke, told by another speaker with enthusiasm and relish and no embarrassment, might have them rolling in the aisles—but if you have misgivings the story will not work for *you.*

Here again, personality is the key. From one speaker a joke can sound funny which, if told by someone else, would be coarse and objectionable.

This applies in trumps to stories with a religious or racial point. Once again the moral is "When in doubt, leave out!" Why send even one member of the audience away undeservedly hurt or disgusted for the sake of one laugh?

There is a fable that women are more restrained than men in their language and jokes. . . . Some are! This myth is reflected in the convention that blue jokes should not be told at a gathering where there are ladies. It is certainly far better to temper your jokes in mixed company than to hint and hint about the kind of jokes you *could* have told, until the ladies take the hint and get up and go out.

I have encountered this kind of thoughtlessness and bad manners and have unobtrusively slipped out and joined the women and some of the men in the hallway outside—where the conversation was much better than the jokes in the dining-hall.

When you adapt an anecdote or a joke to your own purposes, you are not really trying to deceive those people out there in the Woodyard—they know very well that you are not on oath.

If you personalise and modernise an old chestnut no one will jump up and shout "Liar!" The practice is just the equivalent of the comedian's "A funny thing happened to me tonight on the way to the theatre."

But personal anecdotes are best. No one can cap them. Audiences seem to relish in particular anecdotes in which you come out on the losing side.

Examples? When I propose the toast to "The Lasses" at Burns Suppers I very often tell the story (tall but true) about the time when I was dancing with a girl and noticed that she seemed glum.

"What's wrong with you tonight?"

"I've bad toothache!"

"Come outside and I'll kiss it all better!"

"Thank you, but I'd rather keep the toothache!"

If you want to use that story, be my guest, but it really happened to me.

A story which is not strictly true but which has earned some laughs for me—"I don't know what I'm doing standing up here speaking to an audience of women. I'm terrified of women. It was my birthday last week, but I take after my father, and if he hadn't been so terrified of women I would have been at least five years older."

New jokes are hard to come by, and are not always the best.

Many a speaker has found that he gets more reaction from the "mouldy oldies" than from carefully polished new jokes. A good example is the tale of the new husband of the much-married actress who said, "I know just what to do, but I don't know how to make it interesting."

I must have heard that worked into the text of a hundred speeches, and laughed each time.

When I am introduced as an expert in a subject I take refuge in the story about the man who went to the psychiatrist and said that his wife believed she was a hen.

The psychiatrist was sympathetic but encouraging. "I can make no firm promises, but it seems the kind of simple delusion I can cure before long."

Then he noticed that the husband looked rather subdued. "You don't seem too pleased that I think I can cure your wife?"

"Oh, I am, I am! But the eggs have been very handy."

I am not an expert on my subject, but I admit that the "eggs" have been very handy."

A story like that tends to put an audience on your side by making them feel "He's really one of us." But beware of the pitfall of patronising. . . .

If you tell a joke and the audience does not laugh, let it go at that. Maybe they enjoyed it, but not enough to laugh out loud. Don't say "Better luck next time!" or "Ah well, I thought it was funny!", or "It went down well at rehearsal." Just get on with the speech, and hope for better luck with the next joke.

It's not important if you "die the death" with one joke. Walking off to the sound of your own footsteps at the end of the speech is much more devastating—but that happens very rarely.

Maybe this book will help to ensure that you never have to leave a platform without being warmly applauded.

The best of luck with your lighthearted speech-making.

INDEX